Unmentionable

Unmentionable

*The Victorian Lady's Guide to
Sex, Marriage, and Manners*

Therese Oneill

LITTLE, BROWN AND COMPANY
New York   Boston   London

Little, Brown and Company
Hachette Book Group
1290 Avenue of the Americas, New York, NY 10104
littlebrown.com

First Edition: October 2016

Little, Brown and Company is a division of Hachette Book Group, Inc. The Little, Brown
name and logo are trademarks of Hachette Book Group, Inc.

The publisher is not responsible for websites (or their content) that are not owned
by the publisher.

The Hachette Speakers Bureau provides a wide range of authors for speaking events.
To find out more, go to hachettespeakersbureau.com or call (866) 376-6591.

Images on pages 28, 31, 36, 41, 42, 110, 117, 140, 141, 144, 164, 169, 172, 174, 212, 260, 264, 276,
283, 284, courtesy of the Wellcome Collection, London. Images on pages 11, 61, 62, courtesy
of the Museum of Menstruation and Women's Health. The image on page 29 courtesy of
User Musphot on Wikimedia Commons. The image on page 58 courtesy of Harry Finlay, the
Museum of Menstruation and Women's Health. The possible Leonardo da Vinci self-portrait
(c. 1513), on page 159, and Sandro Botticelli's *The Birth of Venus* (c. 1486), on page 288, are
courtesy of Wikimedia Commons. The *Harper's* May cover on page 238, published April
1896, is by Edward Penfield. All other images are in the public domain. Special thanks to the
Library of Congress, Wikimedia Commons, the Boston Public Library, the British Library,
the Museum of Menstruation and Women's Health, and the Wellcome
Collection.

ISBN 978-0-316-35791-3
LCCN 2016937207

10 9 8 7 6 5 4 3 2 1

LSC-C

Book design by Fearn Cutler de Vicq
Printed in the United States of America

To Mrs. Diane Prichard.

Because in seventh grade I said I would dedicate my first one to you.

And I think you believed me.

Contents

Contents

Unmentionable

"YOU"

Hello, Slattern

*T*hank you for coming. Please, won't you sit with me a moment, my friend?

I hope you'll forgive my familiarity, but I do insist on a certain amount of comfort and openness with my traveling companions. A journey of this sort is an intimate affair.

You've come to see me because you have heard of what I can do. Where I can take you.

You are a devoted fan of simpler times, I suspect? You can't resist any film where the heroine wears petticoats, lets her long, beautiful locks fly away from their tight bun in dramatic moments, and calls her father "Pa-PA!" when defying his choice of husband for her.

You think you know the nineteenth century well, as a place of chivalry and honor, gilded beauty and jolly servants. You've been there before, many times, but only as a guest, an observer. Dark-eyed Heathcliff has obsessed over your windblown soul in a universe where no one ever has to poop. You've been to the brightly lit ballrooms swirling with sumptuous silk dresses; you've watched clean-shaven young men contain their smoldering passions and ladies parry their advances with clever repartee.

And you have reason to believe I can draw back the veil of time even further? Well, my darling, you are right. I *can* take you there. I can make the past so real it will bring tears to your eyes.

But I cannot promise they'll be happy tears. A lady cries for lots of reasons. Frustration. Disappointment. The biting stench of the slaughterhouse when the wind shifts.

Most of the things you love about the nineteenth century aren't real, child. They're the curations of gracious hosts who tidy up the era whenever you visit through art, books, or film. You see only the world they want you to see.

But, if you take up your own residency, as I propose we do, the truth cannot be hidden for long.

And the truth, dear, is even better.

Come with me and we will vanquish myth. I'll be your tour guide to the *real* nineteenth century.

I will tell you what you must know to survive. I'll teach you about toilets, or rather the desperate lack of them, and more important *what you're going to do about it*. I'll show you how to bind and cloak your wobbly bits enough not to be arrested for solicitation, and how to conduct yourself in society so as not to be sent to the ice baths of an insane asylum. And I worry that the modern world has allowed you to forget how to properly interact with the opposite sex. Since relating with men is going to be about the most significant part of your life here (whether you like it or not), I'd like to give you a refresher course.

Because if you tour this world as your twenty-first-century self, you will suffer. If you dress comfortably, talk freely, and spend your accustomed five to twenty minutes on your personal appearance every day, you'll be what we in the nineteenth century call a "slattern." A lazy, boorish, miserable waste of womanhood.

And we don't want that, do we?

Oh, you could try to imitate what you remember from books and movies, taking your cues from Miss Scarlett or Miss Bennet. But they merely showed you the guest room of their world, a world where a man needed only to gaze in a woman's eyes to have his heart snared for life, and no one ever had heavy-flow days. Imitating them won't help you find where the housemaids keep the nineteenth-century version of Super Flow tampons. They won't be next to the toilet, dear, because now you dangle your bottom over an open pit,

"What are you staring at?"

or pot, to do your business. And for that matter, pads will be tricky, too, because for some reason all your underwear is crotchless. You've watched every version of *Jane Eyre* ever made and there was never a single scene explaining *that* to you.

But I will.

Of course you must be amenable to some simple rules of travel.

Rule number one: I am capricious and omnipotent.

That fairly well covers it, actually.

I will be transporting you geographically, temporally, and through stages of life and levels of society without continuity or warning.

That way we can absorb as many of the fun, important bits as possible.

You will arrive in the nineteenth century in the guise of a young woman of some wealth, European descent, and living in either America or Western Europe. This is not *remotely* reflective of the experience of most women during this period. Poverty, war, and abuse stalked the earth, and women got the worst of it. In fantasies of olden times, we all tend to picture ourselves as the heroine, conducting our drama draped in a silk shawl and hand-embroidered linen nightgown. In reality, it's much more likely you'd have been born either the slave who picked the linen's flax, the Native American displaced to plant it, or the near-blind, starving seamstress who sewed the finery by the light of a dying candle.

Although this journey will mainly stay within the boundaries of the later Victorian era, I will occasionally include information and images that come from before or after Her Majesty's reign, 1837 to 1901, the better to broaden your experience. Or just because it pleases me.

Do you want to know what is happening to your stately and spirited heroines when the curtains are drawn, when the scene fades to black? Do you want to explore the world that lies just outside the frame? You do, darling. I can tell. Most books and movies give you the foam, delightful and aromatic. I have brought you the bitter dark brew underneath. It's strong. But once you develop a taste for it, you'll never again be satisfied with just the fluff.

Getting Dressed:
How to Properly Hide Your Shame

"Only to think, Julia dear, that our mothers wore such
ridiculous fashions as these! Ha! ha! ha! ha!"

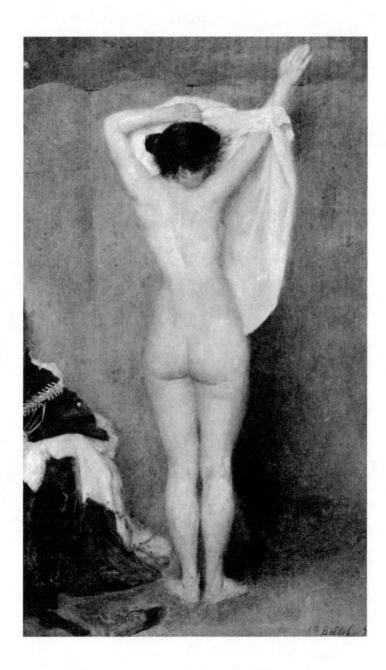

*N*o time to waste. Open your eyes. Awaken into your new life. You're in a sparsely decorated bedroom. The sheets are rough to the touch, the mattress hard, the air so chilly it shows your breath. And someone has left a pot of cold pee under your bed.

You've arrived, dear one. The year doesn't matter, nor the precise place; you don't have time to wonder at the details. You're expected downstairs. We must begin our lessons with haste.

So let's get you dressed, shall we? Pull off that surprisingly coarse linen nightdress and you'll be standing bare and shivering in your bedroom. Don't worry; you'll soon be wearing more layers than a five-year-old on a snow day.

Open your armoire and see if you can find some underwear. Back in the twenty-first century, you loved your underwear, didn't you? Whether you were sunk snug inside your granny panties, or rocking a sexy Saturday-night bra held together with only a scrap of red lace and pure sexual magnetism, they felt good. That which wobbled was bound comfortably and pleasantly presented; that which might leak or smudge was assured an extra layer of modesty.

I'd best break it to you early: you're going to be wearing a lot of things under your dress during your time here—but none of them will have a crotch. Your privates are going to be traveling unaccompanied today. Under miles of fabric, to be sure, but with a direct line of sight to the floor.

Ever wonder why the saucy, high-kicking can-can dance at the Moulin Rouge was so popular? It wasn't because the dancers were showing their stockings, or even their legs.

"Madam, I don't mean to alarm you, but I can see your ankles."

You have a bare bottom for good reasons. You will be wearing very heavy, long skirts that you'll never have cause to lift above your ankles. (Unless a good wind comes and flips your crinoline over your head. And if that happens you'll have to move to a new town and change your name.) So you risk no exposure. Why would you need a crotch? (Well, one reason periodically comes to mind, but we'll cover that in another chapter.)

To really understand how terrific it is to have nude nethers, we have to finish getting you dressed.

So put on your chemise. It's a lot like the nightgown you just took off, except lighter, wide-necked, and short-sleeved. It's actually quite pleasant. If you were back in the twenty-first century, you might wear it as a fun, simple sundress to a summer barbecue, or Shakespeare in the Park. However, if you do that here in the nineteenth century, you won't even have to worry about moving to a new town. You'll be safely tucked away in a sanitarium, where you will be strapped into frigid ice baths and given fantastic doses of opium until your hysteria abates. Remember, the center of a woman is her uterus. Her crazy, crazy uterus.

Now, even though we're leaving your lady parts free to sway in the breeze, we still need to cover your legs. The bottom part with stockings, of course, knitted and held up with garters. What covers the rest of your leg varies over the course of the century and could include pantaloons, bloomers, chemilets, pantalettes, leglets, or Turkish trousers. They're all basic upper-leg coverings worn under your chemise, tied at the waist. And until the end of the century, the legs don't connect to each other at the top. They're left split, with a slight overlap for modesty.

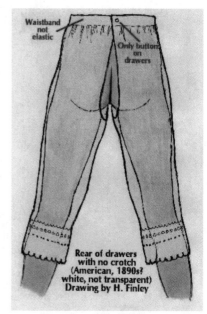

Open drawers

So, chemise, stockings, garters, and crotchless pantalettes. You are still practically naked. All your wobbly bits—there they are, just wobbling. That won't do.

Oh, how you'll miss your cherished bra collection on this journey. Work bras, sports bras, date-night bras, and the fraying, soft-cupped "I'm not leaving this couch until I've watched every single episode of *Downton Abbey*" bras. Brassieres won't become popular until the 1920s, and even then they'll be about as supportive as two kerchiefs tied together with wet paper. For now, dear, we're going to truss you up in your corset!

You've seen the X-rays of ribs grotesquely crushed by years of corset use, haven't you? Isn't it awful? Those horrid stays (the straight vertical strips that give the corset its power and shape) are made of unforgiving steel, or the nearly-as-unpleasant whalebone (actually whale

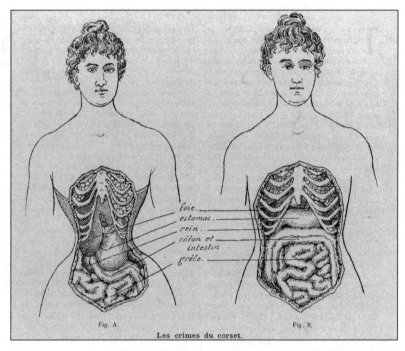

Les crimes du corset.

"I'm serious, Martha. If you don't do something to trim down that elephantine rib cage of yours, you'll never get a man."

baleen, but no matter). How are you going to breathe? How are you going to bend over? How are you going to move at all?

Once you are assisted into your corset (back-laced or front-hooked, sometimes both), you'll discover something. Corsets aren't that bad. They don't *have* to be tightened to the point of spleen displacement. They can function as legitimate support garments, holding up your bosoms, perhaps even putting off the inevitable day when they will lie exhausted and battle-worn against your belly, flapping like tired little beaver tails with every step you take.

For women are fleshy creatures, and many of us feel more comfortable when that flesh is secure. Corsets, like the Spanx and bras of the future, provide privacy. Privacy that women are willing to sacrifice a little comfort for. In the twenty-first century, if your bust was drooping and your bottom flat and wide enough to shoot pool on, you could arrange your clothing to keep that information to yourself. But now, dear traveler, you don't have the option of flowing blouses and jeans made of fabrics that were originally developed for astronauts. You have a corset. And it works pretty well.

As for breathing and bending over, there are smaller, shorter corsets that can provide a working woman some support while letting her scrub and sew her

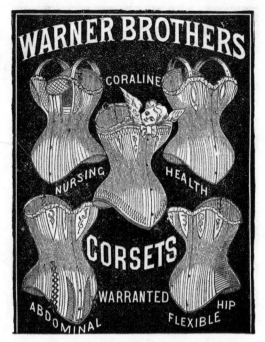

Corsets were available to compensate for every grotesque flaw, including pregnancy

way to an early grave. (Your chemise is clean, by the way, because one of your maids spent an hour dunking it in near-boiling water and lye, until her hands cracked and burned, then wringing, hanging, ironing, and starching it. It isn't uncommon for even a small household to take two days to get the washing done.) A woman who is not of the working class doesn't have much reason to bend over in the nineteenth century. And if she does, a lady lowers herself, straight-backed, by bending her knees. She does not stick her posterior in the air like a common prairie dog.

Oh, look! Your maid has laid out your dress! This is precisely why you chose this travel destination. What a lovely frock. Such exquisite

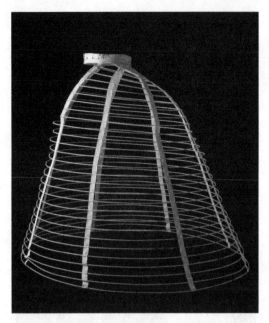

Cage crinoline, circa 1865

embroidery and hand-stitching. Such a voluminous skirt! No! Not yet. No touch. First, put on a loose shirt over the corset. Corset covers prevent everyone from seeing the outlines of your underpinnings.

Now, fetch the cage!

Cage crinoline, that is. You've happened to land mid-century (for now), during the hoop-skirt craze, where the simple flowing dresses of the Regency (think Jane Austen) have been replaced by the biggest, loudest bell-shaped silhouettes this side of Notre-Dame Cathedral. Yards upon yards of heavy wool have been used to construct your dress. To hold it up, you need to strap on your cage crinoline. It is precisely what it sounds like: a wire cage suspended from your hips or shoulders, over which your skirt will rest. These cages, which in their naked state are indistinguishable from something you trap wild dogs in, have a sensible use. Without one, you won't be able to walk.

The cage structure distributes the incredible weight of the fabric and holds the hem away from your feet so you won't trip. Well, you're probably going to trip anyway, because you're wearing forty pounds of clothing, your shoes are crazy pinchy, and there is an amazing amount of horse poop in the street. But it won't be because your dress is too close to your feet.

Now we add a petticoat or six, depending on how much ruffle you need to meet this year's fashion, and hurray! You're ready to have your maids tug your dress over your head and button you up. You look lovely, dear. Which makes me almost not want to tell you how uncomfortable and smelly your dress actually...you know what? We can just wait on that for a bit. You look lovely.

And now we return to the first question you asked yourself this morning as you looked through your undergarments: "Why don't any of the forty-seven pieces of clothing I'll be wearing have a crotch?" Well, let's do this.

Let me sneak you a pair of your old bikini cuts to wear under everything else. No one will know. In fact, wear them to the ball tonight! There you'll be, having a lovely time dancing, eating delicate bonbons, and trading even more delicate bons mots. You won't even care how thick the stench of body odor coated with heavy floral perfumes is. (Bathing, you will soon learn, is a huge pain in the butt in the nineteenth century. Thick perfume is so much easier.)

Now, run upstairs, squat over a chamber pot, pee really quick, and run back down to the party.

Yes. Hoist up that enormous poundage of wool, steel, and cotton with one arm and then pull down your underpants with the other. Go on.

The dangers of the crinoline cage

You fell over, didn't you?

Yes. And by the time you're all buttoned and laced up again, everyone will suspect you left the party for some other more embarrassing reason, like kissing the stable boy, or diarrhea.

That is why your dainty bits aren't covered. Because even though no one in Victorian society will admit to it, a lady has to pee, and "closed drawers," as they will eventually come to be known (because you "draw" them up and down!), make that practically impossible for a fully dressed lady.

Crotches will come together slowly as the century winds down. First buttons will appear, and then finally crotches will be sewn up altogether. This will most likely be due to the extreme narrowing of skirts that becomes popular by the 1880s. Crinolines will bundle themselves up into bustles, which are a lot *like* crinolines—just for your rump instead. A lady will not only be able to raise her skirts, but she will once again fit into her outhouse, although that may not be necessary, as most upper-class families will install indoor plumbing around the 1890s.

Speaking of which, it's time to learn how to navigate your new potty options. I believe you'll find them far more creative and numerous than you'd ever want them to be.

Bowels into Buckets:
Nature Is an Obscene Caller

*How much poorer history would be if there hadn't been so
many artistically talented perverts in days gone by.*

I want you to look at your nineteenth-century shoes. We wouldn't call them shoes today.

They're boots, made of black leather and usually ascending half-way up the calf, fitting closely, with a hard wooden sole. Once you

wedge your foot into them, they are fastened by means of tightly spaced buttons, which, if you are in the unfortunate position of ever having to dress yourself, are freakishly difficult to manipulate. So difficult that a special hook has been invented to make it possible. By modern standards these shoes should be placed next to the fuzzy hand-cuffs in the window of the kind of store that sells edible massage oil.

Fashionable, yet uncomfortable enough to keep your gal from wandering

So why don't you see if you can find some-thing a little less daunting to wear on your feet today? Oh, there's a darling pair! Delicate color, small and sweet. Your maid insists they are mere-ly "house slippers," but they look like the closest thing to actual shoes available. What sort of slippers are made of kid leather and satin, any-way? They aren't even fluffy.

Now, out you go on the town, in your prim but chic little slip-on shoes!

Hello! Back so soon?

Venetian silk slipper

Oh, heavens. You descended your front steps and landed directly in a pig wallow of "mud," which you're pretty sure is 90 percent horse excrement? Oh, poor child! Deep down you know that's not just from horses. Come, now. Don't delude yourself, darling, it just makes this journey harder.

The nineteenth century is so, so dirty. Whether you're rich or poor, living on a farm or in the city, you are going to be ankle deep in filth wherever you go.

Filthiest. Century. Ever.

Some would argue that the nineteenth century was one of *the* filthiest times in all of Western history, particularly in any urban, developed area. Worse than when humans squatted in caves picking lice off each other. (By the way, you'll probably still have to do this on occasion. It's where the term "nit-picking" comes from. But, take heart, not in a cave, and to squat or not will be entirely at your discretion. So there's that!)

Ankle deep in filth, I said, but forgive me, I was inaccurate. You will wish the filth terminated at your ankles. Foulness is *everywhere*. Grime and rot cling to the very air, the buildings, the people; even the soap is made out of lard and poison.

There is no such thing as "fresh air" in the larger cities, unless the winds are blowing it in from other locations, usually at such an icy speed that the fresh air poses a greater threat than the miasma it displaced. There is no electricity and little available in the line of "clean burning" fuels (whale oil burns exceptionally well, but since you still possess a twenty-first-century conscience, you are a heartless monster if you use it). Yet every home and business needs energy, so you must

Flea Crush. Way better than playing Candy Crush.

burn something, like wood or coal. Burn for heat, burn for light, and burn for steam power. The result is the soot and smoke of hundreds of thousands of fires saturating the sky.

And these fires don't produce a charming campfire smell. Though if they did, it wouldn't matter because even that wouldn't come close to masking the *other* smells. Remember your street, stretching before you, filled to the horizon with sewage, rotting offal, and other garbage? Life requires people to perform actions that create waste. And like the smoke that hangs above your city, the more solid pollution is there because it has nowhere else to go.

Regarding the fetid road sludge we'll have to call mud: one of the reasons it is so bad is that most of those streets weren't engineered; they simply appeared as they were needed. Many American streets started out as deer trails, and deer aren't known for ecological foresight. Such streets lack all those little whispers of design and maintenance that would send runoff to gutters and ditches to be carried away. Instead the runoff forms pools and collects in holes of stagnated, polluted "water."

In summertime the mud won't be such a problem, unless it's a wet summer, and then, well, malaria. (A French surgeon will be awarded the Nobel Prize for discovering the disease is caused by mosquitoes that congregate around stagnant water—but that won't be until 1907, much too late for you. So *really* watch out for mosquitoes.) In summer you will have dust, endless choking dust, kicked up by every horse and

Particularly tidy Boston alley, 1890s

carriage that passes. *Bup bup bup!* No. Don't bother starting in about cobblestones. Yes, they exist, and they help somewhat with dust and sludge, but I am not setting you down in any of the places that have them because most places don't and frankly you've already been cut enough breaks on this journey.

Now back to general filth in your new romantic life. Some things contribute more heavily to the problem. Take the issue of sewage treatment.

There is no sewage treatment.

There are sometimes conduits that sort of *feel* like sewers. Streets and a few municipal pipes dump all matter of soggy refuse into these tunnels, and the tunnels in turn carry the awfulness far, far away.

Well, not so far.

Actually, to the nearest large body of water. Which is usually located right in the center of town. Like the Thames, the Seine, or the Hudson. By 1860, the Thames, for instance, was visited by thousands of tons of fecal matter every day from all the pipes and runoffs that emptied into it. Imagine the smell on a hot day. Then get over it quickly because the smell is *nothing*.

The smell isn't the problem. The problem is that these bodies of water and their thoroughly polluted water tables are also where urban residents get their drinking water. For much of the nineteenth century, doctors didn't even know what germs *were* and certainly didn't think deadly invisible animals could exist to a fatal capacity in water, like so many tiny rabid unicorns.

People died because of this. By the thousands they died, from cholera, dysentery, typhoid. Diseases that occur when your body desperately tries to flush unwelcome bacteria from its digestive tract, usually killing you by dehydration in the process. Especially when your loved

Death patrols the Thames, which is filled with refuse.

ones try to soothe your thirst by giving you more poisoned water.

Dirty water didn't even enter people's minds as a source of illnesses. They believed that bad air caused disease, which at least was an improvement on the previous century's obsession with removing "bad blood" from dying patients by the half-gallon. And some Victorian doctors still do that, so pick your physician wisely. Actually, don't—don't go to physicians.

You know better, dear. You know that it would be wise during your visit to stick to coffee and alcoholic beverages, because their methods of preparation kill bacteria. Now let me tell you *why* you know that.

There was a man, beautifully named given his influence on our world: Dr. John Snow. He treated cholera victims daily, breathed the same contaminated air, but never got sick. He was breathing their *air*, but he wasn't drinking their *water*. He drew a map of all the cholera victims in a certain neighborhood of London and noticed that all the worst outbreaks were centered on one thing: a single well pump. A

"The outhouse is there, the slop water is there...just to keep things sanitary we better dig the well between them."

dirty one, contaminated by sewage. Even stranger, there was one place in that neighborhood that suffered no cholera at all. And that was the brewery, where employees were apparently allowed to imbibe their own stock as their main beverage of the day.

Dr. Snow retaught the world something it must once have known instinctually but had been forced to forget in order to survive overpopulation.

Do not poop next to where you drink.

And so midcentury, sanitation reform began in most major cities of the Western world. Better sewers, better garbage disposal. Cities began employing enormous task forces to keep their streets from being hell pits of disease and squalor. Which...ehh...helped?

But our twenty-first-century senses would still be assaulted. There were still limited disposal options for garbage, and endless smoke choking the air. Sanitation reform also couldn't change the fact that most people still needed to use outhouses, pit toilets, and latrines for their daily evacuations. Something you are going to have to get used to also.

The Lady's Toilette and Her Thunder Mug

I know you've come a long way, and no doubt one of your express intentions was to be in a place where people did not discuss their bodily functions in casual company. And now here you are again, listening to your (nineteenth-century version) mother complaining about how "her toilet" took an exceptionally long time today. You might as well have just stayed in the twenty-first century and endured the same discussions with her via cell phone.

But stout hearts, now. "Toilet" means something different here. We appropriated our word for the modern plumbing fixture from the French, who said it more like *twa-lette*. It came from a word similar to "toil," that is, to do work, a job. A "duty," or "doody," one might say.

Ah, heavens. I'm sorry. Punning is the very lowest form of humor, and I do apologize.

Until well into the twentieth century "a lady's toilet" was her beauty routine, the work she did to make herself presentable before facing the world. Then one day, that included pooping in an indoor flushable basin, but no lady wanted to say that, so it simply became part of her "toilet." Then, the success of the appliance caused such a *large, powerful movement* that it just took over the word. (I'm sorry. I'm very cross at myself.)

All humans, always, have striven to remove their bodily waste far from the areas where they did the rest of their living (except when

Two outhouses behind a school in West Virginia.
Considered "poorly placed."

overcrowding—see above—made that impossible). This removal was mostly done by one form or another of burying. Technically that's all an outhouse is: you dig a hole, fill it with the horrid unspeakableness that comes out of your body, and then, when it's near full, top it off with dirt and move the building itself to sit over a *new* hole. Nature agreed with this process: in just a few months' time human waste becomes nearly indistinguishable from the surrounding soil.

No one liked outhouses, particularly house-proud women. Ladies did the best they could, within their means, to make their privies bearable. Still, the "Necessary" showcased everything a nineteenth-century woman wanted to pretend wasn't there, from stinking cesspits right down to the unpleasant headlines on the newspapers that she'd carefully cut into squares for her family to ink their bums up with.

Very wealthy folks had managed to find ways to poop inside for centuries. Even regular folks tended to Nature's disgusting call indoors when they could, usually at night.

Chamber pots, also called the pot, jerries, nightsoil, commodes, slop jars, close stools, and thunder mugs (plus a dozen more charming descriptors that contain language a proper lady should try to avoid hearing in this century), had been lying under beds for centuries. We've actually never totally gotten rid of them. It's just that now they're plastic and have happy animal characters that sing "You're a super duper pooper!" when used, and we call them pot(ty) chairs. Incidentally, it was tiny rumps that were the leading cause of the puzzling two-seater outhouse. Grown-up-size holes could be fatal to children. Plus, rural families had significantly more children than we do now, and parents would have felt no compunction at sending them out en masse to use the facilities before bed, which, by the way, they also shared.

Many of us must still undertake personal interaction with feces. Any parent knows the screw-lipped breath hold involved in dumping out a two-year-old's tiny but offensive poops from potty to toilet. But imagine having to do that for a houseful of people, for grown men who drank more beer than water, and in a time when food conditions were such that you were near guaranteed to suffer diarrhea on a household scale a few times a month.

And imagine *not* dumping it into a sparkling magic fountain that makes all the horribleness disappear in one cleansing whoosh. No, imagine carrying it out to the outhouse with all the care you'd use in transporting sweating dynamite, and dumping it down that grievous hole, wondering if this would be the day levels had risen high enough to cause splash back. There were households in antebellum slave-holding families that found the task so repugnant that they actually *paid* the slave who had to perform such an odious task, Thomas Jefferson's among them.

The more sophisticated placed their chamber pots inside squat little chairs with lids that you could close, providing one more layer of decency and odor protection between you and your dirty secret business. These were called close stools. Because they were stools you sat upon with lids you could close. Now, the next time your doctor requests a stool sample, you can give him some, plus a fascinating bit of etymological history.

An original stool sample

Some fancy folk even moved their stools into separate little closets, for convenience and privacy. Those closets weren't new, really. If you tour the ruins of European castles, you will often see a closet-size outcropping protruding from the wall where the most senior members of the household slept. That was called a garderobe, and you will note that the stone beneath this outcropping bears different erosion patterns than the rest of the wall, the result of centuries of urine and feces splashing down the side of the castle into the open latrine or water source below. It's how almost all your favorite Disney princesses would have relieved themselves. When you return to the twenty-first century, perhaps you can use this information to move your daughter more quickly along through her tragically deluded princess phase. Then tell her Aurora and Snow White and Cinderella would have also hung their best dresses in that same little room, believing the combination of their acrid old pee and the "fresh air" coming up the toilet seat would kill vermin.

That ought to scoot her right into her infinitely more pleasant horses and Harry Potter phase.

Winning the Right to Be/Receive Number One

People seldom pooped down the side of their walls by the Victorian age. The idea of a private, separate room for your foul expulsions had reappeared, however, and it was here, in this little room, that a great battle was waged. In the late nineteenth century, two popular kinds of toilets were taking the Western world by storm. But only one would emerge victorious. The two contenders: Water closets (toilets that flushed with water) and earth toilets.

Moule's earth toilet

The Lambeth "combination" water closet

Earth toilets were invented by a man named Henry Moule. He found outhouses abhorrent and refused to own one, demanding that all the people in his household use chamber pots, the contents of which would be buried nightly in a faraway ditch. Moule came up with the patent for the earth toilet, a device intended to add comfort and sanitation to that same process of disposal.

Earth toilets were a sensible option—inexpensive, simply built, and requiring no sewage system or even a real cesspit. People simply did their business, which landed in a large bucket. They then pulled a handle, as you would to flush, except this pull brought down a layer of dirt, ash, or quicklime that completely covered both the sight and odor of the bucket's contents. At the end of the day you'd be able to carry your tasteful little bucket of people-litter to an appropriate disposal pit (where it would soon turn into safe and reasonably fertile dirt). It sounds disagreeable to us, but the people of the nineteenth century were used to dealing with human waste, and to have it pleasantly pre-buried while in transit was quite acceptable.

But alas. Once Victorians felt the thrill of looking down after a rush of cleansing water crashed from the cistern and carried away all signs of their beastly humanity, leaving gleaming white porcelain behind, the soddy old earth toilet didn't stand a chance. The prospect that, aside from a bit of squat and dab, they might never again have to handle their own feces was just too appealing. So the water closet, which soon expanded to contain all the new plumbing fixtures invented to make humans less disgusting, was born.

Paper Work

Humans have been producing excrement for thousands of years, so we had plenty of time to hone the science of wiping. But toilet paper, in its earliest recognizable incarnation (softish, disposable, made singularly for undercarriage maintenance), wasn't commercially marketed until 1857. It was called hygienic paper, and it wasn't an instant hit. Why spend money on something you intended to wipe your rear with and throw away? Take out the middle step and you're literally throwing money down the pooper.

Toilet paper as *we* know it—rolled, perforated, and making a real effort to not feel like a fistful of bark chips—was introduced by the Scott Paper Company in 1890. They didn't want anyone to know it was them, however, and sold their product directly to pharmacies and stores through subsidiaries, who in turn sold the disgraceful item from under the counter. It takes courage to be the first family to have your name emblazoned on a product designed for dirty bottoms. Courage that the Scott family eventually showed in the early 1900s.

This convoluted ad served as a coupon of sorts:
you could hand it to your pharmacist and receive the toilet paper in return
without ever having to make eye contact.

So, since toilet paper was barely present in the nineteenth century, what did folks use? In the United States, corncobs and newsprint were the favorites. Most Americans had farms, or at least kitchen gardens in which to grow corn. The bare cobs were stored, usually soaked by the batch to soften them, and put inside the privy. They were porous and well shaped for their job. Catalog pages and newspapers were also good options; their paper was thin and plentiful. Often people would hammer nails into the wall of the outhouse and hang all manner of scrap paper there for later use.

Early French bidet

The European continent went in more of a wash than wipe direction, placing special pitchers and sponges within easy reach of the toilet basin so people could straddle and douse their naughty bits clean. A now-extinct small, sturdy horse breed called Bidet may have been the inspiration for the name that came to be attached to this device.

What else did Victorians use to cleanse themselves after evacuations? *Whatever worked.* Leaves, rags, even sticks. None of which, I promise, will you need to resort to while visiting. I took away your cobblestones, but I will leave you the yielding pages of the annual Sears, Roebuck catalog.

3

The Treacherous Art of Bathing

"If you didn't want old drunks busting down your door to leer at your naked body, why did you take a bath in the first place, you sly wench?"

*N*ow, then. Have you come to terms with the knowledge that your new home is in a society so unclean that the very water flowing from the earth causes an appalling yearly body count? If you have, you'd probably like some tips on how to keep clean!

Oh, you won't keep clean.

At least not by twenty-first-century standards. Gracious, no. Even at your best you'll feel like you've just slithered in from two weeks spent camping over a natural sulfur deposit. But you can maintain hygiene acceptable to the standards of the era. And you should. Being dirty kills. There are reams of scientific-ish material on the subject.

Consider the explanation of how filth causes illness, published in 1847's *Chambers's Edinburgh Journal,* volume 10:

> "The scurf-skin [dead skin, or dandruff] is being constantly cast off in the form of minute powdery scales; but these, instead of falling away from the skin, are retained against the surface by the contact of clothing. They also become mingled with the unctuous and saline products of the skin, and the whole together concrete into a thin crust, which, by its adhesiveness, attracts particles of dust of all kinds, soot and dust from the atmosphere, and particles of foreign matter from our dress."

You are a magnet for every airborne poison, disease, and blind gypsy's curse you encounter. Thus your other organs—lungs, kidneys, liver, and the like—must overextend themselves trying to compensate for how disgusting you are. They *will lose.* Says *Chambers's Edinburgh Journal,*

There is simply no excuse for being dirty. Usable water is a mere three-mile walk away, and you own at least two buckets.

"The Oppressed organs must suffer from exhaustion and fatigue, and must become the prey to disease. Thus, obviously and plainly, habits of uncleanliness become the cause of consumption and other serious diseases of the vital organs."

It's time for a bath, dear. We must save you from your own repugnancy.

Bathing has to be done very particularly. And in this era, doing something right often means doing it as uncomfortably as possible. Otherwise it might appear you're taking pleasure in unwholesome activities, which are pretty much anything that doesn't include bracing morning walks and reading the Old Testament. And *taking pleasure in your own body,* well—you're obviously not reading the right parts of the Old Testament reverently enough if you think that's acceptable.

Bathing styles here vary with social class and geography. Most people prefer not to bathe everything at once, unless it's summer, because the warm air means you'll be less likely to die from bathing. Wetting the whole body at once strips it of its natural defenses and is sure to result in derangement, raving fevers, and consumption. Until later in the century, when wetting the whole body at once will become the *cure* for those conditions.

Sponge baths are a popular option, but not the kind of luxurious sponge baths administered by an attractive nurse of your preferred gender. No, you give them to yourself, standing nude in your own freezing bedroom or water closet, usually with cold water and a touch of vinegar or some other additive intended to make the experience less pleasant and more wholesome. Victorians favor sponge baths not just for their cleansing properties, but for the good hard burnishing they involve, invigorating the blood that *eeks* through your freezing skin. (Do not perform these ablutions in a warm room. It will lead to torpor, masturbation, and, like everything else in the nineteenth century, consumption.)

Bath temperature is a point of serious contention. Even women authors, or at least authors claiming to be women, join the chorus of caution. Mrs. A. Walker, authoress of 1840's *Female Beauty, as Preserved and Improved by Regimen, Cleanliness and Dress,* weighs in on the mind-rending terrors of hot bathing:

> "Nothing is more likely to awaken many irritations, than baths taken at too high temperature. The effects of a hot bath are evidently debilitating. The body loses too much in such a bath.

Baths heated to above 110 degrees have lately, in several instances, been known to produce immediate insanity."

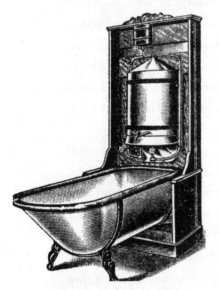

See the little water heater on the wall? That's where the depravity comes from.

Interestingly, 110 is a popular temperature for modern hot tubs and Jacuzzis. As we now know, such vessels do frequently induce a kind of insanity, causing people to strip themselves of both morals and swimwear and dive headfirst into fleshy madness laden with regret. I daresay Mrs. Walker saw that coming.

Oh, but the cold bath, though it feels painful and pious, can be just as detrimental. Says 1833's *The Toilette of Health, Beauty, and Fashion,* written by an anonymous expert (as a great many beauty and hygiene books were during this era) and published in Boston by Allen and Ticknor:

"Considered as a cosmetic, the cold bath possesses no virtue whatever; it renders the skin hard and scaly; and this induration of the skin may prove injurious to health, by checking too suddenly the insensible perspiration."

Scaly skin, resulting from cold bathing, prevents proper perspiration, promoting poison pores. Precisely. Whereas:

"Warm baths contribute greatly to the preservation of the complexion, by giving freshness and an exquisite color to the skin. Hippocrates recommends the washing of children with warm water, to protect them from convulsions, to facilitate their growth, and to heighten their colour."

Hippocrates was brilliant. He was also dispensing this health advice over two millennia before the publication of Allen and Ticknor's book. He claimed that menstruating virgins risked having blood build up in their heart and lungs, causing sluggishness and insanity. Which, actually, hasn't entirely been disproved by this era…

Moving on. Let's say you are a lady of wealth in the latter part of the century—a lady in need of washing. You go down the hall and step into that most modern of conveniences, the indoor bathroom. Immediately you are confused. There are so many kinds of baths. Foot baths, hip baths, full immersion baths, shower-baths, and douches. No, not what you think.

In twenty-first-century French, *prendre une douche* still means what it did in nineteenth-century English: to shower. It had medical overtones then, but not specifically the medicine of the vagina. As described in the 1879 *A Treatise on Hygiene and Public Health,* volume 1, edited by Albert Henry Buck,

"The douche consists in a stream of water, varying in size and force, applied at a greater or less distance against different parts of the body. The douche exercises a certain amount of friction and a continuous pulse on the spot to which it is applied. It quickens the circulation, and is said to favor the absorption of various diseased deposits. Its effects are so powerful that it cannot be applied for a long time."

Left to right: foot bath, hip bath, plunge bath, sink, shower-bath (or douche bath).

Eventually the necessity of pulse and friction to remove "diseased deposits" lessened, and the douche treatment evolved into something more familiar. The douche streams were mounted on walls and became, in English at least, "showers." Meanwhile, using a very specific "continuous pulse of water" became a fashionable way for ladies to maintain intimate cleanliness. Ladies clung to the French word, however, to bring dignity and that ever-popular French mystique to the activity. How much more pleasant to murmur "Tsk-tsk, *mon amour. Je vais prendre une petite douche*" with a whimsical wink when your lover asks where you're disappearing to than to say "I will now flood my vaginal canal with water in hopes of rinsing away offensive odors and foreign bacteria. Stud."

Which brings us to another form of bathing, one that will not survive long into the twentieth century—the sitz bath, or hip bath, which is a bit like a porcelain (or tin, depending on your finances) bench in which you can sit, with only your fundamental bits submerged. In an era when filling a tub is an exhausting undertaking and sponging a freezing and filthy business, the simple sitz bath is a revelation. It attends directly to your most troublesome parts with minimum fuss and is a godsend for menstrual and postpartum hygiene.

But no one will say that out loud. So instead the sitz bath is recommended for infirm persons, who can be comfortably sponged off without having the deadly

That acne represents some serious disease deposit. You should have face-douched more.

pressure of a full bath compressing their sickly chests and giving them consumption. But really the point of the sitz bath is to provide quick, soothing sanitation to the dirtiest division of your personage. You can rinse away whatever the Sears catalog has not wiped and, by adding the right ingredients, provide spot-on treatment for chafing, hemorrhoids (called piles), and the bevy of venereal diseases your husband brings home.

Now, bathe *safely*.

According to *A Treatise on Hygiene and Public Health:*

• Certain precautions must always be exercised in bathing of whatever sort.

*"Oh, I don't know, Clara, are you sure this is safe?
I just ate some filberts."*

• The bath should not be taken "on an empty stomach"—that is,
when one is conscious of being hungry—or when one is fatigued.
Nor should it follow a meal too closely; three or four hours
should be permitted to elapse.

• The proper time for bathing is in the morning, either before
breakfast or about noon.

- A good reaction is a necessity to the advantageous use of the bath; unless the bather feels a "glow" after the bath, "it has done him no good and possibly may have done him harm."

You're Going to Stink, But You Can Choose Your Stink

Just a quick reminder, darling. Though you are keeping yourself as clean as you can, deodorant and antiperspirant have not been invented. Not until 1888, anyway, when a potted paste called Mum hits the market, designed to be dipped into and applied with your fingertips. It's slow to reach the masses, though, so don't hold your breath. Or rather, do hold your breath.

You (and everyone else at an indoor summer cotillion or in a crowded streetcar) will use perfumes and colognes. And scented face wash and scented talc powders and lavender-flavored breath lozenges and heavily perfumed hair pomade. These will be much heavier scents than you're used to; Victorians favored strong, alcohol-heavy floral aromas over the sweeter and crisper perfumes we prefer today. Because *we* want to smell sweet and fresh. *They* wanted to drown out the horrid stench of their own humanity. Yes, the odors may be noxious, but at least it isn't your own private flesh smell that's making the gentleman next to you queasy. How distastefully intimate that would be.

Washing Hair. Or Not. Whatever.

There is no consensus on the proper way to clean your hair. In 1881's *Sylvia's Book of the Toilet: A Ladies' Guide to Dress and Beauty,*

Gentlemen: when you're about to put the moves on your gal, who will probably let you, judging from the amount of skin she's showing, don't forget to "perfume the breath" with lavender lozenges.

Sylvia (the pseudonym of a person who also wrote books instructing ladies in macramé and profitable church bazaars) suggests you begin your hair-care routine in the same manner the modern fertilizer industry begins creating *its* product: with a good heavy rock of pure ammonia.

> "Pour upon [the ammonia] a quart of boiling water; when cool enough to allow of the hand being put into the water without the slightest discomfort, beat that member about in the water until a lather is formed. With this rub the roots of the hair all over the head, and then the hair itself....Take a basin full of warm water

President Buchanan's Inaugural Ball, 1857. That's the stench of victory, friends.

and wash out all the lather. Then a douche or two of cold water, after which the head must be thoroughly rubbed until the skin glows."

Ammonia becomes highly corrosive when reacting to water, which would probably be very effective at stripping hair of grime. Also skin of its superfluous top few layers. As for getting the remaining skin to glow, that won't be hard, since ammonia destroys cells, including blood cells. Like the sort found in your skin and lungs. Oddly enough, frequently breathing in ammonia gas, though so acrid it is painful to inhale and a definite contributor to lung damage, was *not* considered a cause of consumption.

Ride as fast as you may, darling, but you can never ride away from your own hair.

Sylvia is one of many beauty experts to laud the effects of onion juice for hair growth. If one finds that smell too unpleasant, because one has forgotten one lives in perpetual stink anyway and suddenly one has standards, she suggests adding ambergris, the slightly sweet, slightly flatulent-smelling intestinal seepage of the sperm whale. Ambergris is a very popular ingredient in cosmetics and perfumes here. It will be illegal to own in twenty-first-century America, because of the sperm whale's endangered-species status (of which the seeking of ambergris and the aforementioned lamp oil was a leading cause). Also it's whale's poop-mucus. Stop playing in whale poop-mucus. Just stop.

And how often should the hair be washed? It all depends on your hair and which expert you consult. Also the environment you live in, the season, and of course the fiber of your moral character. An immoral girl is a greasy girl.

Truthfully, with the exception of the general "not often" rule, the standard for hair washing is, again, whatever works.

Scribner's *The Woman's Book* (1894) recommends a wet washing about once a month. Don't use soap, which will give you dandruff. Eggs, whipped and smeared about your hair, are a better approach. Do you rinse the egg out? Oh, who knows. It hardly makes a difference at this point. No matter what you do, your hair here will not be the hair you're used to.

Our friend Mrs. Walker has her own opinions.

"Supple moist oily hair may be washed every eight days with luke-warm water. Light hair, which is seldom oily, and the fineness and soft-ness of which obviates the use of pomades, rarely requires washing."

If the lice come on extra strong, a little vinegar and lard caked on your scalp should suffocate them out. Also there is a possibility they dislike...parsley? So mix that in? Or it might have been paprika. An-ise? Nobody likes anise.

Frankly, you can forget the whole thing as long as you're diligent about brushing. And one more little secret. Instead of washing your hair, says Mrs. Walker, try this: "A little honey dissolved in a very small quantity of spirit, scented with rosemary, &c. is an excellent substi-tute."

It also might attract malaria mosquitoes, so be careful. And when all else fails, go with the nuclear option. Perfume that mop with pun-gent chemical concoctions until the tears in people's eyes make their vision too bleary to judge cleanliness.

White Washed

In the war on nineteenth-century personal putrescence, there's one more battle you must prepare for. You came here for the clothes: the swooping femininity, the elegant lines, the delicate fabrics. But how will you keep these beautiful gowns looking their best?

Now you know why all your shoes are leather boots, made of ma-terial that can be easily reblacked or rewhited. And now you see why men of all stations favor dark colors in their wardrobe, to better hide the accumulation of unavoidable dirt. So why is it that, besides the

boots, the finest pieces of *your* wardrobe seem to make no concession to the barrage of contaminants that beset you from all sides? No, your beautiful dresses aren't dark or plain. They're vibrant, patterned, plumed, and begging for attention.

Well, "begging for attention" is perhaps a little much. Now might be a good time to notice the difference between real "fine dresses" of the era and those created by artists working in oil paints or Hollywood.

Only trollops and the foolishly wealthy dress showily. But you mustn't be afraid to add a little color and embellishment to your pretty frocks—dirty roads, air, buildings, and other people be darned.

Victorian women knew that their voluminous dresses were difficult to keep clean. That they remained so was an important testament to their delicacy and careful natures. Your clothes must tell the world that you are spotless, in habit, form, and soul. And that you seldom have need to engage in self-sullying activities, like cleaning, cooking, or reading a newspaper that might leave ink on your pink and perfect fingers.

Especially since you will never, ever wash that dress.

You can't, really. The fabric is too delicate for the boiling lye, plunging, scrubbing, and wringing of the day. There is too much lace and too many embellishments, and although clothing dyes are the boldest and most adherent they've ever been, anything but a light spot-clean will deaden the shade of even the most well-dyed fiber.

Victorians didn't like to wash their outer clothing. That's why they wore so much *underclothing*.

"My heavens! How lovely! A 'wringer,' you say?
Is it for punishing the servants when they are insolent?"

A1047 *Late for Breakfast*
copyrighted by William H. Rau

She may be a dirty girl,
but her linen is white and clean.

White linen (for the wealthy) and white cotton (for the poor) were very popular fabrics for undergarments precisely *because* they showed any bit of spoilage. In fact, some people thought the material itself motivated the body to self-clean, sucking the unhealthy elements right out of you in the form of sweat stains. Those clothes were washed much more often.

An especially confident person might even wear white outer garments, like those favored by Puritans centuries earlier. One of the reasons you see so much white in lace, aprons, cuffs, and collars in old paintings is because, since they were nearly impossible to maintain in that condition, they were a subtle way to signal the wealth, immaculate personal habits, and piety of the subject.

You'll have a handful of tricks to help you keep your dress clean. You may attach the train of your dress to your wrist with a little loop bracelet. You might have a sort of dust ruffle, called a balayeuse, that lies under your hem, secretly separating it from the ground it drags upon.

Dress and cape with extensive balayeuse

As for keeping your dress free of offensive odors—that just isn't going to happen, bless your heart. You will air your dress as often as you can. Maybe you'll get an aerated closet in which to hang your dresses, hoping that the exposure to fresh air will make them less stinky (no urine fumes required in this advanced age). You can also use dress shields, half-moon shapes of absorbent fabric that separate your non-

Alpha dress shields, 1902
Sears, Roebuck catalog

deodorized, hairy armpits from your clothing.

Oh, and yes, you are hairy. Everywhere. There is no such thing as a lady's razor, although there are many depilatory "creams." These are chemical suspensions that eat up the keratin protein in your hair. And your face, which is also mostly made of keratin protein. Most of these depilatories, while not explicitly revealing themselves as skin smelters, do recommend only the briefest contact between them and the human body. They are used *only* on the face, hands, and arms. No other hairy bits will be shown until the 1920s.

All in all, I wouldn't worry all that much about the state of your hygiene while you're here. People in this era do not disdain body odor or hair that lacks silky bounce as you've been conditioned to. Embrace hygiene as much as you need to feel comfortable, especially when it comes to our next topic: how to menstruate in the nineteenth century.

4

Menstruation:
You're Doing It Wrong

*N*ow gird your loins, dear ones, as we approach one of the more delicate subjects of our study. Actually, don't bother. You're going to need full access to your loins here.

From a very young age, Queen Victoria sat on one of the most powerful thrones in history, overseeing the largest empire on earth. And she sat on that throne without any money-back-guaranteed leakage protection. Can you imagine having to take on Prime Minister Robert Peel and all his insufferable Tory cronies *without* super-absorbent confidence?

Have you ever looked at the covers of your mother's trashy romances and wondered if those women were pushing away their kilted, oily-chested lovers not because of deep rivalry between their equally

sexy clans, but because it was her time of the month and she didn't want his greasy man-breath anywhere near her?

As much as it spoils the romance of history to know that women of old struggled with aching ovaries and slipping fabrics, they did. If it's any consolation, their "monthlies" spoiled things for them, too. So they said (and wrote) very little about it, dealt with it as best they could, and got on with life.

It was quite revolutionary when, around the mid-1800s, male doctors developed a fascination with menstruation. They began to study the process. Though in most cases the gentleman's knowledge was so complete, and the woman's ignorance so apparent, that study and research were moot. In any event, they realized, not a moment too soon, that women had been menstruating incorrectly. Many a man became determined to teach all of womankind to achieve their full menstrual potential.

It's Natural, But You're Still Probably Sinning

Women and girls probably did not menstruate as often in the nineteenth century as they do now. For one thing, girls began their periods later in life, in their midteens, as compared with today's twelve-year-old average. *Good* girls, that is.

George Napheys, in his 1888 edition of *The Physical Life of Woman: Advice to the Maiden, Wife and Mother,* warns that a menstruation begun too early is detrimental and that she who develops early fades early, with a "feeble middle life." And what causes the curse of early menstruation and the overripe sexual disposition that accompanies it? Well, any number of unwholesome indulgences. Attending the theater, having a childhood crush, and, most damaging of all, music.

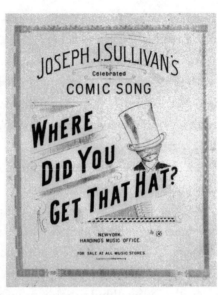

"Whatever stimulates the emotions leads to an unnaturally early sexual life. Late hours, children's parties, sensational novels, 'flashy' papers, love stories, the drama, the ball-room, talk of beaux, love, and marriage,—that atmosphere of riper years which is so often and so injudiciously thrown around childhood,—all hasten the event which transforms the girl into the woman. A particular emphasis has been laid by some physicians on the power of music to awaken the dormant susceptibilities to passion, and on this account its too general or earnest cultivation by children has been objected to."

Absolutely. Top hits of 1888 included such lascivious titles as John Philip Sousa's "Semper Fidelis" march and the painfully overt "Where Did You Get That Hat?" Where, indeed. From the devil's quivering loins, most likely.

No matter when your "monthly unwellness" came in life, it could still be counted on to visit less often than your twenty-first-century period. Poor nutrition and a harder physical life contributed to scanty menses. And with no standard birth control, a married woman could spend a great deal of her life pregnant or nursing, which stops or at least reduces menstruation. Also, people tended to die more often, and younger, which was also factored into these kind of statistics, though I'm not sure it was fair to do so.

But when it *did* happen—what did they do?

Whatever Holds..."Water"

I'll tell you what they did. They did *everything*. Or they did *nothing*. I *think*.

One of the reasons we know so little about how ladies controlled (or didn't) their menstrual flow is because no one wrote down the details. The topic appears in literature of the past centuries in one of two forms: the absolutely baffling medical/hygiene treatises we are about to explore, and in the most unsettling of pornography. The world-renowned deviant the Marquis de Sade barely touched on it in his literary tour of sexual hell, *The 120 Days of Sodom*. Because even a man so depraved that his very name still stands as the definition of sexual torment (sadism) simply could not bring himself to go there.

As for women themselves, few even knew how to write until the latter days of the nineteenth century. And when they did write, they didn't waste paper and ink on compositions that began: "O my dear Abelard, the cloth I hath fashioned round my womanly fount doth bunch most vexingly."

Stories beginning "I remember Grandma once saying..." form the

Nineteenth-century Norwegian crocheted sanitary napkins.
Because winter was long and very dull.

bulk of our knowledge, supported by a scattershot of recorded observations.

From various reliable sources, here are the methods of nineteenth-century menstrual hygiene available to you during your stay here:

- Nothing. Clothing was dark. Some experts, including Harry Finley, the curator of the brilliant online Museum of Menstruation and Women's Health, and many of his learned colleagues, believe women simply bled into their clothes, particularly rural women and pioneers. (The nothing method is still practiced in many countries.)
- Sheep's wool, fluffy side up, after applying lard to the vulvar area to protect against dampness.
- Raw cotton, wadded, secured in cheesecloth, and inserted like a tampon.

- Sea sponges, applied in the same fashion.
- Homemade belts, made out of anything that could be tied around the waist, from leather to string, attached to any reusable pad, forming a T bandage, named for its shape. Most pads, homemade or store-bought, were about the size and texture of a folded hand towel. The pads were run the length of the crotch, belly to back, and safety-pinned (invented in the 1840s), buttoned, or tied to the belt.
- "Clouts"—little cloth triangles with attached strings to tie around a woman's thighs and waist.
- Crocheted sanitary napkins, attached to a belt.
- No belt or support at all. Ladies with thick enough thighs some-times just placed towels against themselves, relying on their mighty farm-woman bulk to keep it stationary.
- Baby's diapers, folded, used with or without a belt.
- Small albino marmoset, clinging tenaciously.

That last one is not real. Probably not. But if my research shows anything, it's that if you should happen to have had a surplus of mellow marmosets and they got the job done, you would have darned well used marmosets.

That's not funny.

Hide the Evidence

There are several unnecessarily complicated explanations for how the expression "on the rag" became a common slang for menstruation.

One is that women tried to fool the male members of their households into thinking the bloodstained cloths soaking in bleach under the claw-foot tub were leftover rags from the making of jams and jellies, never mind that jam making took place only once or twice a year. This might have been the practice in some homes, but even the most slovenly woman would not have wanted her menstrual blood needlessly on display every time someone came in to use the Necessary. Others talk of "rag bags" where women collected the last tattered remnants of household fabrics, which were then portioned out for flood control. And from a global perspective, rags were at the fancy end of the spectrum; women from non-Western cultures used grass, moss, papyrus, anything that could be counted on to hold an ounce or two. *Anything that worked* was what women used.

At the end of the century, commercial feminine protection became common, especially since the increasing popularity of mail-order catalogs allowed a woman to purchase it without causing the local pharmacist to suspect her vulgar addiction to menstruation. Reusable *and* disposable cloths were suddenly available, and waterproof, stain-shielding "sanitary aprons" formed a secure barrier between your clothing and your impudent menstrual blood.

Of course some women chose neither store-bought protection nor any of the simpler homemade solutions. Women who were not afraid to put a little flair into their flow could create garments to rival any of today's options. A German publication gives instructions on how to origami yourself yet another wonder of Teutonic engineering. See the illustration on page 62.

Toward the end of the century, when cloth was easier to come by, what happened to menstrual rags after they had served their purpose was an interesting indication of wealth and social status. A lady of rea-

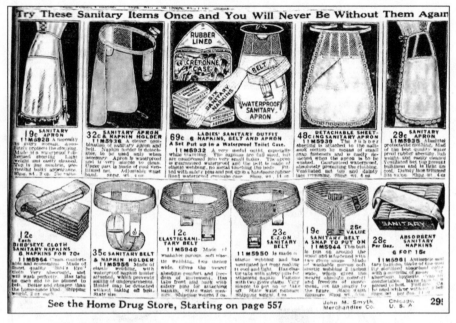

Your late-nineteenth-century armory against the Red Baron(ess)

sonable wealth could afford to toss her soiled rags, purchased from a catalog for that singular purpose, into the outhouse pit. She wouldn't even have to let her maids in on that particular vulnerable evidence of her humanity. The maids themselves, however, like most of womankind, still had to wash and reuse their own cloths. The main problem with that being, once these rags were cleaned, they had to be hung up and dried. Where?

Not on the clothesline, that's for certain, unless your home adjoins an abattoir and you can pass them off as tiny butcher's aprons (you would never, ever be able to completely bleach a reused sanitary napkin back to whiteness, and there would be no mistaking its true nature). And not over the fireplace either, for these reminders of the

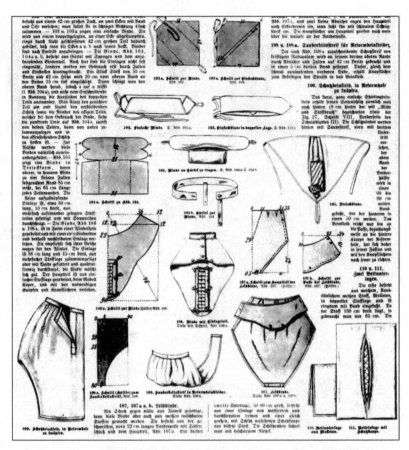

*From an unidentified nineteenth-century German publication,
a page entitled "Underwear for Special Times"*

curse of Eve were hidden from all members of a household who didn't use them. Even if you were alone during the day, you couldn't be sure a neighbor wouldn't call at your door, watching you through the window as you pinballed around your parlor, hiding menstrual rags like a meth head during a police raid.

Therefore, should you happen to catch a glimpse through a neigh-

"Oh, no! A knock in the darkness! It could be a murderer! He'll see my jelly rags!!"

bor's bedroom door of a drying rack set with menstrual cloths, you would know that particular family practiced frugality, either from sense or necessity. And they would know they have the kind of neighbor who peeps in bedrooms. Show some dignity, darling.

Trifling and Tuberculosis

While published advice on controlling the actual menstrual flow was scarce, advice on how to *conduct* a menstruation cycle was impressively vast and plentiful, and donated to the female gender almost entirely by men. Men wrote books teeming with tips on what a woman should avoid, what her menstrual blood indicated about her health and character, and the many dangers that awaited her if she did not expel her uterine lining with the greatest of care.

Pye Henry Chavasse, who wrote *Advice to a Wife on the Management of Her Own Health* (1880), was just one of many male doctors with opinions on this subject. He shared the popular belief that certain activities, foods, and drinks could take an already troublesome situation (bleeding from your vagina) and make it lethal. Biggest culprit: cold water. Which was most of the water in the nineteenth century.

"During 'the monthly periods', violent exercise is injurious; iced drinks and acid beverages are improper; and bathing in the sea, and bathing the feet in cold water, and cold baths, are dangerous; indeed, at such times as these, no risks should be run, and no experiments should, for one moment, be permitted, otherwise serious consequences will, in all probability, ensue. 'The monthly periods' are times not to be trifled with, or woe betide the unfortunate trifler!"

Hattie's menstrual-trifling high jinks always got the girls laughing.

I'm not even sure how one would go about "trifling" with her period. It's not an activity that lends itself to festive sidetracking. "Oh, gracious, I know I should use a good absorbent napkin and diligent cleansing for this—but the heck with it! This month we'll see what just cinnamon sticks and doilies can do!"

According to Chavasse, nearly all cases of hysteria, a disease both powerful and not actually real, can be traced back to uneven menstruation.

Most of these men were not stupid. Their medical educations (if they had them) did enable them to know more than the average woman about the unseen functions of her body, same as today. These men had never menstruated, but that in itself does not disqualify their advice. I don't demand to see a troublesome mole on my physician's buttock before allowing him to examine mine.

What does disqualify their advice is that it came mainly from studying incompatible animal biologies, corpses (often of people who'd died from disorders of the organ in question, making their anatomy nontypical), and abashed women seeking help only when they were suffering (again, presenting a nontypical representation).

Probably Chavasse wasn't thinking about that when he made such declarations as that all menstrual blood, through the entirety of the cycle, "ought to be of a bright red colour, in appearance very much like blood from a recently cut finger." Any other color or texture, he warned, was a sign of endangered health.

> "If [the menstrual blood] be either too pale (and it sometimes is almost colourless), or on the other hand, if it be both dark and thick (it is occasionally as dark, and sometimes nearly as thick, as treacle), there will be but scant hopes of a lady conceiving."

As most women know, even if your menstrual discharge flows in a rainbow of shades from near black to pink, you're probably okay. For women to think otherwise could be very frightening for them. Because according to science ("Science." Oh, that's fun. Let's call it that!) many horrible diseases came straight from wrongly colored period blood. Sterility, of course. But also tuberculosis.

> "The pale, colourless complexion, helpless, listless, and almost lifeless young ladies, that are so constantly seen in society, usually owe their miserable state of health either to absent, to deficient, or to profuse menstruation....How many a poor girl might, if this advice had been early followed, have been saved from consumption, and from an untimely grave, and made a useful member of society."

"Makes Her Most Ugly and Hateful"

The quantity of your menstruation was also important to your general health, as we learn from Orson Squire Fowler, whom we shall revisit many times on our journey, as no other writer can be relied upon for such potent truth bombs as he. Fowler was already an old man when he wrote *Private Lectures on Perfect Men, Women and Children, in Happy Families* in 1880. He wasn't remotely a doctor. Well, he was a phrenologist. A word that *sounds* doctor-y, but many words do. Like "timbrologist," which is an old word for stamp collecting, a pastime that holds as much medical influence as that of phrenology. But he had a *lot* of ideas. About everything. From octagonal houses to marital relations to improving farming methods. And of course, like any educated gentleman of the Victorian age he had ideas about women's periods. His theory regarding menstruation and tuberculosis was slightly more developed than Chavasse's. Imagine an old man shouting the following information at you:

Fowler. Orson Squire. Remember the name.

"Spare menses cause and aggravate all diseases, by leaving surplus albumen [a blood protein, similar to what makes up egg whites] in its victim's system to create pains and humors. Nature must rid her of it somehow, else she dies, and so burns up in her all she can, which fevers and morbidizes her nerves and feelings, unfits her to bear, and makes her most ugly and hateful, especially to men, and often fairly insane against her husband; besides sending her thick blood tearing through her brain, torrent-like, to gorge, lacerate and soften it...if the lungs are strong enough to help, a part is pressed out from the blood through into their air cells, which she coughs up and raises easily, with difficulty if she has consumption, of which she dies if they cannot do both; so that raising by the gallon proves their strength, and is her salvation."

"Unclench, woman! Your very life depends on it."

Did you get all that? You have been retaining your menstrual protein. Probably because you're pouting. Stop this foolishness and let the blood come out of your vagina—or it's going to dice up your brain and choke your lungs. And frankly, with the attitude you've been sporting, no one is going to miss you.

Fowler's solution for sparse menstruation was to lie in bed with all available blankets covering you and apply a towel just taken from boiling water to your abdomen. Then remove the blankets and place a near-frozen towel on yourself instead. Repeat until the blood in your sluggy, disagreeable midsection is galvanized into motion. Also helps with constipation.

No Baby Angers Tetchy Uterus

But *why* must women suffer so? Most nineteenth-century health reformers agreed that although God decreed that woman should have pains in childbirth as penance for original sin, He never actually cursed a woman to suffer during her monthly cycle. Therefore, if your monthlies were unpleasant, it was probably your own fault.

First of all, if your period is not regular, if it is not uniform in shade, and if it does not pass from your uterus as easily and pleasantly as poetry from your lips, the doctor will ask, "Are you married?" Because if you aren't, it's obvious that Nature finds you abhorrent and is just trying to let you know.

From Stewart Warren's *The Wife's Guide and Friend* (1900):

"Many of the irregularities of menstruation in single women such as scanty or absent, painful and profuse menstruation…are often cured by marriage, and are in such cases nature's sign to a woman that she is not leading a natural life."

Try to imagine your uterus as a highly strung, frantic woman. Which is pretty much how all these writers are imagining it, so you might as well. Anyway, Uterina can't stand being bored. She wants challenges. She wants work to do. She wants to toss around eggs and play sperm soccer and engorge herself with waterlogged humans four times the size of herself. It's okay! She's made for that! She craves it!

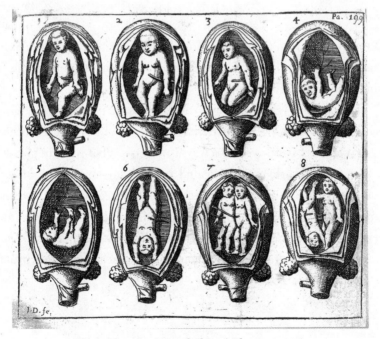

Nature's way: jazzy babies in happy uteri.

And you, who are *unnatural*, who are perhaps too busy sewing the ridiculous sashes your fellow Sapphics wear while throwing themselves under carriages in a diseased effort to procure suffrage, are foiling her needs. She will see that you pay for that crime: punishment meted out from the very organ you neglected.

Or, bless you, you just might be terribly plain and dull-minded. And no man wants to extend the effort of shoving a ring onto your hoof. In which case I am so very sorry and I'm sure, should you give enough of yourself to doing good works, you can distract yourself from poor fallow Uterina and the agonizing monthly tears she sheds for your sorry state.

The Indian Girl and the Negress: The Lucky Ones!

Do you suffer from cramping? Bloating? Fatigue? Headaches? Well, that's what you get for having a reasonable allotment of human rights, a housemaid, and a full tummy.

Take it from James Craven Wood, who says in his 1894 *A Textbook of Gynecology*, "Menstruation should be as painless and as normal as defecation." Well…yes, in a way, I suppose. That wouldn't be the first analogy I'd use, but then again I am not a doctor. The point is, if your menstruation pains you, it's partially because you didn't have the fantastic good fortune to be born a woman of color in the nineteenth century. Your darker-skinned sisters are having a fine time of it. *They* were blessed with the marvelous constitution that accompanies brutal relocation and forced labor.

Says Wood,

Some girls have all the luck.

"The Indian girl, and, we are told, the Negress in her native abode, do not suffer in the least, notwithstanding the fact that at all times they are subjected to the most severe exposure and exercise. Their systems have become inured to hardships by the environs, which have exerted a hardening influence, not only upon them, but upon their ancestors through countless generations.... The influence of hard work and simple fare upon the quantity of hemorrhage is incontestable. The girl or woman reared properly and endowed with a constitution such as she is entitled to as a birthright, can stand exposure during menstruation which would be decidedly hazardous to her more delicate sister."

Wood's basis for this theory is stated clearly in his first sentence, "we are told." And that's as good a chunk of medical research as you're going to get, missy. Citing sources was not considered nearly as important in this era. I think Mark Twain said that. Or Lincoln. Somebody.

Menses Don't Lie

Many doctors and probably a few farmers and a handful of very intuitive carp of the nineteenth century believed your menstrual flow was directly connected to your personality. Your behavior and attitudes would actually *create* your physical condition. So, if the previous two problems (unmarried and delicately Caucasian) did not explain your difficult menstruation, there were still a variety of personal failings to consider.

In an 1889 edition of the homeopathic medical journal *The Hahnemannian Monthly,* a Dr. B. F. Betts suggests medical treatments for various illnesses of the uterus. He details what sort of women are associated with different menstrual cycles:

Menses delayed or scanty: A woman who is often suicidal, tainted by syphilis, nervous, and "has light hair."

Menses too frequent and too profuse: A woman for whom thinking too hard will trigger blood flow, found in "fat, flabby, and scrofulous [run-down-looking] patients."

Menses irregular: "Weak, nervous, languid; desire to remain quiet."

Menses that cause vertigo and ringing in the ears: "Weak, delicate women who perspire easily and are very susceptible to draughts of air."

Menses offensive, acrid, too frequent, and too profuse: "Fat and
anemic, apprehensive, timid, unable to sleep after 3 a.m."
Menses very dark: "Nervous women."
Menses dark, thick, profuse, and exhausting: "Haughty women, who
treat their friends and equals as inferiors."

In conclusion, women are just awful,
and periods prove it.

One redeeming note about all of these
publications is that although men took
it upon themselves to tell women how to
manage their offending bodily functions,
they all insisted it was a mother's duty
alone to tell her daughter of the coming
change in her body. Without exception,
they railed against the "foolish modesty"
that stayed a mother's tongue and left a
girl believing herself deathly ill with no
one to turn to, since she'd been taught the
foulness of even thinking about that part
of herself. Doctors told of girls stuffing
their private parts with freezing snow to
staunch the flow they thought fatal. Only
a cruel mother would allow her beloved
child to endure anguish like that, they
concluded.

*Look out, boys. Lotta's
headin' into town and Aunt Flo
is ridin' shotgun.*

We should leave the business of menstruation on that peculiar high
note. It's comforting to know that these educated and, one might even
say, preposterously confident men believed there were some things in a

woman's life best learned from other women. Of course men still had to remind the silly darlings of their duty to instruct younger women about these intimacies. But now that we know just how horrific a woman's monthly sickness actually is, we can hardly blame her for being a bit skittish and absentminded, can we?

5

Diet: You're a Little Bag of Pudding

Don't Be Fat.

I Want to Prove to You Before Your Own Eyes and at My Expense That I Can Reduce You to Normal Weight Safely, Without Starvation, Diet or Tiresome Exercises.

It Doesn't Matter What You Have Tried Send For This Free $1.00 Box of My Safe Fat Reducer Today.

"I Know From Personal Experience There Is No Longer Any Excuse for Anyone to Be Too Fat. Try Kellogg's Safe Fat Reducer, As I Did," Says Ada Rayner.

*L*et us say that one of the many reasons you've sought this romantic century is because you are rather on the fleshy side. And you are tired of always being on the outs with modern fashion. You've found yourself in tears in dressing rooms; six pairs of jeans crumpled on the floor, each more hateful than the last. Your own mother once told you, "Patterned leggings are a privilege, not a right." You just know it's going to be different here.

Examine the newest style of pannier or bustle designed to make a rump look big, and then throw back your head and laugh. Nature endowed you handsomely in posteriority. You used to rue Her for this. But now, ho ho! Tsk at the advertisements offering cures to fatten ladies up. Imagine needing a potion for such a thing. Bosom-growing cream? No need! Your own fine flesh can fill out the generous girth of your corset's bust quite sufficiently.

Finally your day has come! A time when men worship a woman of curves and flesh! Where to be well fed and sedentary is a mark of health and wealth. Finally, fat is in fashion!

Yes, my little dumpling. Get all of that rejoicing out of your system.

Deep breath, now, my girl. I'm so sorry. It's not true. Fat isn't fashionable in this century. In fact, since beauty adheres to such a narrow standard during this time, it's probably more deplored than in the twenty-first.

It's *plumpness,* dear one. A very specific, healthy, youthful *plumpness* that is adored here. No one wants to look heroin-chic in this era; that much is correct. People here associate prominent cheekbones and flat chests with hunger, sickness, and, of course, sin.

Remember Mrs. A. Walker, writer of *Female Beauty, as Preserved and Improved by Regimen, Cleanliness and Dress*? She has firm opinions on this matter, naturally. (I should probably tell you, though, that a *Mr.* Alexander Walker was also writing a lot about women's beauty around this time. They're either married or he's pretending to be a woman to sell more books.)

Says "Mrs." Walker:

"Yes, I've an even distribution of fatty tissue that makes me both sensually soft and fine breeding stock. Why do you ask?"

"A total want of roundness of form, a yellow skin, hollow and livid eyes, sunken cheeks, nose shrunk so as to be absolutely ridiculous, the mouth fallen in, and the neck lengthened and showing all the subjacent parts, are the effects of extreme thinness, with which, however great the regularity and beauty of the features may be, it is scarcely possible to be less than hideous."

And how did she get that way? Either physical labor, excessive thinking, or vice. It doesn't matter which; you want nothing to do with women who dabble in any of those activities.

"More frequently, however, it is owing to violent or long continued exercise or labour, to bad choice of food, salt, spiced or bitter, to unwholesome water, to indulgence in vinous or spirituous liquors, to hot and dry air, to excessive mental application, to violent or sorrowful passions, to abandonment to pleasures, protracted vigils, &c."

All of this would seem to indicate that more ounce of bounce is desired, yes? No.

A certain Helen Jameson, who, though she may be brutal, can never be accused of being patronizing, lays it out plain for us in her 1899 book, *The Woman Beautiful.*

"It is better by far to be the butt of jokes concerning 'walking shoestrings' or 'perambulating umbrella cases' than to waddle through life burdened to death with an excessive amount of flesh.

"Sigh...being beautiful is such a curse
when it makes all the uggos and fatties jealous..."

The thin sister can pad out the angles, put frills and puffy things over the bony places, but alas for the fat one."

Alas! Look at the art of the day. The women, though often more rounded than those in our twenty-first-century magazines, are nonetheless perfect hourglasses. Their figures are similar to those of our plus-size fashion models. That is to say, opulent but lithe, perfectly proportioned in beauty and poise, long-legged and small-waisted. You know, genetic freaks.

I'm so sorry. I wanted it to be true, too. But the fact is, even a firm stoutness is considered maternal and fusty. You must pursue nearly the same standard of beauty that plagued you in your own century. Diversity and deviation from the norm are not celebrated; they're not even tolerated. Your imperfect figure is just one more way you're disappointing yourself, your community, and your God.

You're a Little Bag of Pudding and You Aren't Fooling Anyone

But surely the styles of the era must help a bit in disguising your unwanted jiggles and flap-overs. I mean, it is no longer imperative that your blue jeans display a bottom the bitty size and shape of two genetically modified ripe blueberries. You no longer risk having a forty-dollar designer white T-shirt become nothing but an expensive sausage casing when it fuses to your back fat for the world to see. All your bumps and bits are hidden beneath your corset and your enormous skirt. Right?

Up to a point, yes. But here comes Helen Jameson again with that crushing honesty:

That's right, Susan my girl.
They're going to gawk no matter what...
so make 'em pay for the privilege.

"Alas for the fat one! She gets into clothes that are skin-tight, and she draws in her corset string until it snaps and gives at every breath and sneeze, and even then she does not look graceful and pretty, for the fat—like secrets—will out, and it rolls over and around like the little bumps and humps in a pudding bag."

And there it is.

Ms. Jameson offers a regimen for reduction.

To lose fat:

Get out of bed, open the window, and breathe the cold air. Cold is a good soldier in the War of Waddle. Speaking of which, now take marching steps, hands on hips, across your bedroom. Then we must chafe and sting your flab, so as to make sure it knows it is not welcome here.

"After airing your lungs close the window and run into the bath-room, where you should have a quick sponge bath, rubbing the body briskly with a heavy towel. A quick alcohol rub can follow."

Her diet requirements are sensible, mostly. No sugar or creams; fair enough. Also never eat bread. Only toast. *Bup!* They are *different.* Toast is dried out. Which is necessary to the girl trying to lighten up because water is a very heavy substance. It's simple logic. Jameson warns against overhydrating: "Do not drink much water. A little lemon juice added to it will make it less fattening."

Unless of course you get your water from a contaminated well. As we have seen, cholera can induce amazing weight loss.

And if you *are* obese, for heaven's sake don't make a further spectacle of yourself by trying to imitate the normals. Martha Louise Rayne, who wrote *Gems of Deportment and Hints of Etiquette* (1881), explains:

> "Ladies who are very stout make objects of themselves by tight lacing, which reddens the face and distorts the figure. If they would wear loose clothes, accustom themselves to breathe softly instead of panting, walk with dignity instead of rolling or waddling, and be unobtrusive in the colors they wear, half of the unpleasantness of too much fat would be avoided."

There is no need to wear fashionable colors or clothing for *you*, my chubby little cherub. Here, I think we have some old bedsheets—dye them black with the ashes of your self-respect and sew them together. Then cut a tidy head hole, and voilà, you've performed a common courtesy to all who might have been blighted by the sight of you.

Poisoned People Seldom Overeat

Now that you've discovered there is only so much a corset's steel boning can suppress, you might begin to consider weight loss, nineteenth-century style. Surely it must be easier than it was in the twenty-first century, for a thousand reasons. No television or computers to keep you inside all day. If you want a cookie, you have to make them, or get up, ring a bell, sit back down, tell a maid to tell the cook to make them, and then wait an hour, by which time your peckishness will have likely passed. Simply everything, even getting undressed at night and then re-dressing for marital romance in a much larger gown, requires dozens more physical actions than were needed in our century.

But perhaps even more to your advantage: the medical community is as of yet very…open-minded about certain substances. Birth-control pamphlets might be illegal, but you can find cocaine in the finest of restorative draughts. I mean, if you really think about it, cocaine

Fat Folks, Take Dr. Rose's Obesity Powders and Watch the Result.

Retail price.................75c
Our price, each........$0.50
Our price, per dozen,. 4.20

TOO MUCH FAT is a disease and a source of great annoyance to those afflicted. It impairs the strength and produces fatty degeneration of the heart, and sudden death results. All people who have obesity are troubled with **sluggish circulation** and labored action of the heart. The patient feels lazy and burdensome. There is a sluggish condition of the whole system; they are not exactly sickly, there is a feeling that all is not right. Nervousness, rheumatism, headache, dropsy and kidney diseases are frequent complications of obesity, and, more cause to be alarmed, the heart is always affected. Send at once for a box of Dr. Rose's Obesity Cure. It will reduce corpulency in a safe and agreeable manner, perfectly harmless. No bad results follow its use, as is the case with many of the much advertised cures. Explicit directions and valuable information for

A boon to fat people who will be glad to obtain this remedy at home when they know you keep it on hand . . . . . .

Fat folks, take Dr. Rose's COMPLETELY NOT COCAINE Obesity
Powder and watch the result WITH A MANIC CLARITY
NEVER BEFORE ATTAINED.

is nothing more than an exceedingly efficient stimulant. Like a brisk walk around the lake on a crisp morning, but in powder form.

Did you know that arsenic and strychnine speed the metabolism? Here in the nineteenth century they are also used in weight-loss medications, though that will seldom be indicated on the bottle. It's *patent* medicine! The ingredients are a trademarked secret! So maybe you won't know that tapeworm larvae fit into pills, either, until you have to pay extra for the deworming medication offered at the end of the regimen. Ideally, you simply allow the worms to grow (sometimes up to thirty feet) inside your digestive tract, which they do by eating a portion of your calories and in general mucking up your digestive process. Then, once weight loss has been achieved, simply take another pill to kill the worm and allow your body to void it. Throw it up? Oh, lambkin. No. It's much too low down for that. You'll have to check for the beginning of its extrusion when you use the chamber pot. Then remove it yourself, by hand. All thirty feet of it. You'll need to pull very gently—you really don't want it to tear.

On the cutting edge of diet pills are the desiccated pig and cow

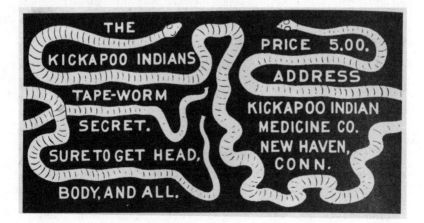

thyroids that seem to work wonders on obesity, as inducing severe hyperthyroidism, what will later be called Graves' disease, will often do. Again, there is no Food and Drug Administration or any other sort of agency to keep "doctors" (they probably aren't doctors, but it's unseemly for a lady to pry) from prescribing these products, all of which can honestly be advertised as "natural," and some even as "purely vegetable." (For instance, cocaine comes from coca leaves in the Erythroxylaceae family—I think that technically counts as a vegetable.)

So however tempting they might be, I cannot recommend you take any of this century's miraculous fat-reduction medications. Weight-loss regimens are just as futile here as they were in the twenty-first century. The potion might work, but it won't last once you stop, and heaven knows what damage it's doing to your body while it's in there. Also, it's made from the same stuff as street crack and rat poison. Dignity, *cherie*. Remember your dignity.

Your Fat, Sluggish Womb Needs Loving

So let us entertain other options. Does Orson Squire Fowler, expert ranter, have any advice? Indeed he does!

Fat, says Mr. Fowler, is incompatible with femininity. In fact, it destroys feminine attributes from the inside out. It takes the magnetism right out of your breasts!

> "Nature turns into fat what surplus albumen she cannot get rid of otherwise; stows it away first right around the womb, thus filling out the belly…then between hips and ribs, making the waist large and back broad: then sends it to the breasts, one of its natural outlets, making them fat, soft, cold, unmagnetic, high and blubbery….Yet this makes her red faced; critics saying, 'Fat and

red faced too, yet always grunting. Humph. Only making a fuss:'
whereas fat, red face and all are due to her spare menses, and this
to her sluggish womb."

Mr. Fowler has previously informed us that a woman's stubbornly
retained menstrual blood would eventually seek escape through her
lungs, leading to consumption. Now we see that if a woman foolishly
retains her menstrual blood by squeezing her woman organs with fat,
the blood will ascend to her face. Which explains the flushing faces of
heavy persons. Oh! It's just too horrible to contemplate. No wonder a
woman becomes, as they so often do in Mr. Fowler's philosophy, "hateful and spiteful to men, in order to drive them from her, because she is
unfit to bear."

Fear not! Good Fowler does not leave us alone in such desperate
straits. He has a long list of advice for the fat woman wishing to reduce. Eat lightly and exercise, which is common enough information.
But a mind like Mr. Fowler's cannot stop at common information. You
must also breathe a great deal, because the "life process" burns fat.
Make sure your bowels and bladder are clear, as well as your skin; you
may not know this, but perspiration "ejects fats" right through the
pores. You must also "promote menstruation." I believe Fowler has
instructed us elsewhere in his writings to accomplish this by not being
so petulant.

But the best thing to do, if you're tubby, is find a man. Remember,
Nature abhors an empty womb.

> "Nurture love if married, and if not, do all you can to get a beau
> and husband; for womb stoppage causes [fat], and action will
> carry off this fat. Stout girls imperiously demand this marrying
> prescription."

And once you've snagged that man, "bear on [have children] as long and often as possible, thus consuming this surplus in the natural way, multiplying life, and keeping up normal womb action."

Imagine that. So many women have convinced themselves that having children makes it more difficult to maintain a youthful figure, when in fact the larger the brood, the sleeker the sow.

"Perambulating Umbrella Cases"

But what if you left the twenty-first century in a slight, slender body? Now you're considered scrawny. You can't get a man if you don't

look like you've got good birthing hips and ample dugs, *ma petite!* We have to fatten you up! Doing so requires a regimen even more severe and difficult than that which your pudgy sister must endure.

Mrs. Walker recommends the "coma victim" approach.

"A female desirous of acquiring fullness of figure must...never incur fatigue, but indulge in the most complete listlessness and inactivity, not in darkness, but in very faint light, in some sequestered, quiet, cool and rather humid place, where the air is bland, where no noise is heard, and where she is not liable to be startled or surprised."

THE "SPÉCIALITÉ CORSET"

Regd. Design No. 2517

IS A **DREAM OF COMFORT.**

Assuming the life of a lichen does not excuse one
from proper corseting.

Being startled triggers harder breathing and beating of the heart, which we know consume fat. And likely causes consumption, because most things do. In fact, any severe emotion can delay weight gain.

> "She [must] avoid all anxiety, and endeavour to feel indifferent to every sensation, reflect as little as possible, and occupy herself with lively and agreeable subjects; shun sitting up, gaming, all strong, afflicting, or turbulent passions, and all excesses; sleep a long time, ten hours at least, and when not asleep, rest as much as possible listless, in dim light, talk little, and indulge in every thing which tends to produce relaxation in the activity of the functions."

Eat fattening foods and don't think, feel, talk, or get out of bed. Well, we've all had weekends like that. Who could have imagined they held such medicinal value?

And remember, chocolate loves you no matter what size you are.

Helen Jameson picks up the discussion sixty years after Mrs. Walker, with more detailed advice.

Personality contributes to body weight. Skinny people, Jameson explains, have more stress.

> "Fretters are invariably thin; they simply worry off the flesh faster than nature can create it."

Well, that was before the Choco Taco, box wine, and full seasons of television shows where strong female cops seeking justice *and* love streamed on demand. That mighty Dame Anxiety has made her peace with food aversion.

So for women who might be strutting their jutting hip bones down catwalks a hundred years hence, action must be taken. They must be cured of their terribly unpopular "barren-womb chic." Jameson agrees that ten hours of sleep is a must. But it must be "healthy sleep in a well-ventilated bedroom, on a hard mattress, and with no high pillows to make her stoop-shouldered and of ungainly figure. A nap during the day is a good thing if one can afford the time." And her diet? Oh, my.

"The diet must be of the most nourishing, and should consist mostly of food containing starch and sugar, such as good fresh butter, rich milk, cream, fruits both raw and cooked, macaroni, fish, corn, sweet potatoes, peas, beans, ice creams, desserts, pastries, and nourishing broths. Cereals, poultry, game, chocolate and sweet grapes are all excellent. Avoid all spiced, acid or very salty foods."

So many rules to remember! Jameson, however, has a final thought about this fat-or-thin issue, and it is a good one.

"Therefore, say I this: Don't worry yourself into your grave about too much flesh or a lack of it unless you find yourself taking on the extreme proportions of a skeleton lady, or a museum exhibit of unusual plumpness. A thin neck may be a bad thing…but if that thin neck is rebellious, and pays absolutely no attention to tonics or massage or other coddling for which it should rightly be grateful, then merely say, 'All right, if you insist!' And turn your attention to other things. What admirer of feminine beauty would not look upon a bright mind, quick, kindly wits, and sweet lovableness as a thousand times more acceptable than a neck as round and perfect as that of a Venus?"

I say, good show, Helen Jameson. Good show!

6

Beauty: Scorch, Slather, and Stuff

*F*ancy clothing filled out by a fashionable figure represents but a fraction of your feminine beauty. We have so much more we must do. Being a woman of elegance is a chore, and it has always been so. Consider cosmetics.

Before the nineteenth century, if you wanted to get dolled up special (perhaps in hopes of attracting the eye of the freshly widowed swineherd as he drove his passel of hog flesh past your gate), you would use ingredients from your own garden and your own dead and rendered livestock to do so.

Case in point is the receipt book (British for "recipe book," past versions of which usually included how-tos for cosmetics and medications as well as food) written by Mrs. Hannah Glasse. In the 1784 edition of her *Art of Cookery, Made Plain and Easy: Which Far Exceeds Any Thing of the Kind Yet Published* (probably a reasonable claim, mostly due to the scarcity of printing presses), Glasse offers a recipe for lip rouge made of hog's lard and beeswax, melted and mixed with the mashed-up root of an innocuous flower called alkanet, all scented with a little lemon. Simple, safe, and hardly whorish at all.

Still, a good woman's conscience may prick at the thought of unnatural augmentations. For her, there is the advice given in a 1794 edition of *The Weekly Entertainer.*

INNOCENCE:—A white paint, which will stand for considerable time, if not abused.

MODESTY:—Very best rouge, giving a becoming bloom to the cheek.

TRUTH:—A salve, rendering the lips soft and peculiarly graceful.

MILDNESS:—A tincture, giving sweetness to voice.

TEARS OF PITY:—A water that gives luster and brightness to the eye.

In other words, the best beauty enhancer is to become an ascended saint, the Virgin Mary herself if possible.

I know. Gag me with a wimple. And so hypocritical. Slathering women's magazines, novels, and advertisements with figures of unattainable beauty is just as common in the nineteenth century as in the twenty-first.

"Makeup? Oh, gracious, no. I look like this because I've never heard a swear word."

Cosmetics were controversial in this era, partly because they were intended to impart the false appearance of youth, which was considered gauche and dishonest. And partly because they were also meant to elevate facial characteristics associated with sexual arousal, such as flushed cheeks, dilated eyes, and reddened lips.

But honestly, I think most of the controversy stemmed from the fact that cosmetics just weren't very good back then. People could tell when you were painted up, all gaudy and greasy, and it probably looked rather, well, *gross.* If your foundation is made from lard and poisoned lead, how flattering can it really be? Still, you must make your own decision. Let's start with a little background information; particularly, the reason most nineteenth-century people have for disdaining a "painted woman."

Jezebel: vicious whore

Esther: righteously indignant concubine

Jezebel Was Wicked. Wicked Delicious.

Most people don't consciously connect sin, deceit, and sexuality to cosmetics. But many do *subconsciously,* even now. This is in part thanks to a biblical character named Jezebel. The word "Jezebel" has a long history of being hissed behind closed doors in reference to women considered too colorful, in both face and reputation. Even today it is still sometimes used as a synonym for a sexually promiscuous or manipulative lady.

Jezebel was an Old Testament queen, the wife of King Ahab, who worshipped the false god Baal. (Ah ah ah...*no*. We shall not debate which gods are false and which ones are true, Ms. Minored in World Religions. On this journey you are in the Western world as a lady of proper society, and therefore there is One God for you, the Judeo-Christian one. All the other options are Satan deluding the unwashed. If you want to be open-minded and inclusive you should have gone to Berkeley, not the nineteenth century.) Jezebel schemed and murdered her husband's enemies and did all that stuff people who want to rule empires do. Basically, she was a real saucy piece of work, though there is no evidence she was ever sexually promiscuous. Except that she wore makeup. It's circular reasoning. Just go with it. She's not so well remembered for being a brutal tactician who refused to change her religion as she is for *this* line, describing her as she prepared for the arrival of the godly man she knew was coming to have her killed:

"She painted her face, and tired her head [fixed her hair], and looked out at a window."

Some think this means Jezebel planned to seduce her way out of this problem; others think she was facing death with composure and dignity.

At any rate, her eunuchs saw that they were on the wrong team and shoved her out the aforementioned window, and dogs ate her face. Which reinforces the assumption that her face was coated in sinfully delicious animal fat.

There are lots of mentions of makeup and adornment in the Bible. Queen Esther, biblical heroine and savior of the Jewish people, was a harem girl, and it took a year of heavy beauty treatments before she was taken on by King Xerxes as one of his favorite concubines. All the while she was lying about her Jewish faith, and when she became queen she asked the king to grant an extra day of bloody massacres and to please impale the corpses of her enemy's sons on poles. Because that's what people did in those days. But Jezebel was on the losing side of history, and her act of gussying up as she prepared to face her death cemented her wickedness, and the wickedness of her beauty regime, in the minds of generations.

So between biblical bad girls and millennia of equally bad ingredients, cosmetics had never been considered entirely wholesome. But in the nineteenth century, science—fresh, mad science—had arrived to add some kick to the beauty scene. And the combination of these two temperamental ingredients was downright devilish.

Men of virtue soon began to take notice of the unholy union. Dr. James P. Tuttle wrote in volume 25 of *The Medical Record* that chemistry was being abused most horrifically by the cosmetics industry for the glory of the morally corrupt.

> "The science of chemistry and art of pharmacy have been exhausted to prepare delicate colorings and bright enamels for the complexion. It seems to have been a conception of the ages past that these adornments added to the personal attractions of men as well as women, inflaming passion and calling forth amorous ebullitions in the opposite sex. That it should be held in disrepute will not be questioned, for it was those whose consciences did not falter at whatever means to gain an end—the vicious and vulgar, the harlots and witches—who were the originators of these practices."

I would not argue with the good doctor, but I would suggest that there have always been women, even a few of spotless character, who want to look young and pretty. Historically, a great deal of a woman's power lay in her ability to please the eye. The only difference in the nineteenth century was that women could now get their pimple cover-up, hair poofers, wrinkle plumpers, and bosom ballooners from a wildly unregulated chemical industry instead of a farmyard. Even without treacherous eunuchs and dogs waiting to eat your face, vanity was dangerous.

A Droopy Bosom Declares a Droopy Soul

Before we start beautifying your face, we might as well spend our initial energies on the area men are going to look at first. We ought to make sure your bosoms are bouncy, pert, and plump. Or, according

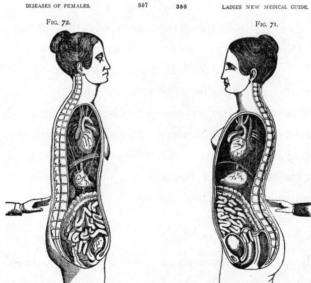
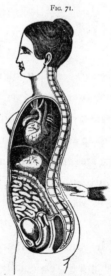

DISEASES OF FEMALES.   357   356   LADIES NEW MEDICAL GUIDE.

Fig. 72.   Fig. 71.

REPRESENTATION OF A RELAXED, DROOPING, AND BADLY-PROPORTIONED FIGURE, WITH THE LUNGS AND STOMACH DRAGGED, AND THE WOMB, BLADDER, RECTUM, AND BLOOD-VESSELS OF THE PELVIS AND LEGS COMPRESSED BY THE FALLING OF THE BOWELS, FROM THE RELAXATION OF THE MUSCLES OF THE SPINE AND ABDOMEN.

REPRESENTATION OF A HEALTHY, ERECT, AND WELL-PROPORTIONED FIGURE. THE SPINE HAS THE NATURAL CURVES, AND THE ABDOMINAL VISCERA IS PREVENTED FROM PRESSING UPON THE WOMB, RECTUM AND BLADDER BY THE ABDOMINAL MUSCLES.

Unhealthy lady with sad bosom   *Healthy lady with cheery bosom*

Pineapple, circa 1890s

to 1890's *Heredity, Health and Personal Beauty*, by John Vietch Shoemaker, "the highest [best] type of bosom...is not only placed well up on the chest, but can be best described as of slightly pine-apple form."

Pineapple. Well, fruit can change over the centuries due to advances in agriculture, so maybe a pineapple in 1890 looked entirely different than—huh. Nope. That's a pineapple, all right.

Of course most ladies don't have the good fortune to be born with breasts naturally squat and spiky enough to qualify as top-notch tropical produce. So we look to the experts. As with other "unimportant" facets of female health like beauty and reducing chubstance, it was the lady lecturers of the era who offer the majority of busty advice. Or at least writers claiming to be ladies.

Mrs. S. D. Power does just that in 1874's *The Ugly-Girl Papers,* a book intended to help women avoid that distinction. The breasts, she writes, must never be touched but with the utmost delicacy. She cautions never to let a well-meaning nurse or nanny rough up an adolescent bosom in an attempt to inspire its growth. Yes, puzzling and creepy by our standards, but—well—actually it was rather creepy to most of them, too.

She explains:

> "It would be unnecessary to say this, were not French and Irish nurses, especially old and experienced ones, sometimes in the habit of stroking the figures of young girls committed to their charge, with the idea of developing them."

Oh, those Irish. This isn't the last time we'll be having trouble with *that* lot.

No, the proper way to fill out those flat figures, says Mrs. Power, is simple cold water—the discomfort of which will stimulate blood supply—applied morning and night, sponging "always upward, never down" (*gently,* for we must not aid gravity in its vicious design).

A different approach was advocated by Lola Montez, a brazen (Irish!) dancer and the mistress of Ludwig I of Bavaria, who made her a countess. In her later years she traveled the lecture circuit, advising ladies on how to make themselves worthy of being a king's bit of boom-boom on the side. She dedicated a whole chapter in her 1858 book, *The Arts of Beauty, or Secrets of a Lady's Toilet,* to the care of the beautiful bosom, for, as she quoted from poet Peter Pindar, "Heaven rests on those two heaving hills of snow."

Montez insists that a girl should not even touch her own developing breasts except when absolutely necessary, and then only with the utmost delicacy. A teenage girl's buddings should be uncorseted, "as unconfined as a young cedar!" (Are you picturing a skinny little tree with bark-bosoms? I am.) To enhance one's bustline, she recommends rubbing the following ingredients on them (*gently,* lest they deflate!), all pretty much just variations on scented water: "tincture of myrrh, pimpernel water, elder-flower water, musk," and "rectified spirits of wine." That should get your bodice seams bursting in no time.

Of course, if it didn't, you could always "stuff." Stuffing wasn't such a desperately childish thing to do back then, as most corset styles flattened what little you had into oblivion. So inserts—basically bust-shaped metal frames made to withstand the pressure—were commonly sold right along with the corsets.

For the lady trying to reduce an *over*abundant bustline, Countess

Corset insert: sooo much better than wadded-up socks and Kleenex.

Montez advises that you not drink iodine, no matter how tempting or fashionable. She suspects it is unhealthy. Rather she recommends rubbing that iodine topically—*gently!* Your breasts are so delicate they make a baby's fontanelle look like a granite slab!

Many women turned to the terrifying world of unregulated patent medicine to embiggen their bosoms. In 1869, an unknown author using the pseudonym George Ellington set out to "boldly and truthfully" unveil the disgusting secrets of females in the metropolis, "where sin and immorality have tainted women in high life, and where fashionable wives and beautiful daughters have yielded to the enticer's arts." Those arts, he warns his readers in *The Women of New York, or The Under-world of the Great City,* included something called Mammarial Balm, a stimulating lotion, or "breast food," that ladies applied to their bosoms and then helped along with suction cups and air pumps until those bosoms swelled. According to Ellington: "A lady makes the application two or three times a week, and in the course of time a breast is developed which suits the taste of the most exacting."

By modern standards, such methods are nothing short of horrifying.

Mostly because we now know how useless they were. It is not my place to dictate what you choose to do to make your body more husband-entrapping—but if larger breasts really are a concern, tend to it *before* your journey here. No amount of "breast food" can match the skill of a twenty-first-century surgeon and a bag of silicone. Mr. Fowler,

Nature has not favored you. Shove your palm in Nature's face and start lathering and pumping.

as an example, wouldn't be fooled by the falsies of the day. That gentleman knows his mammaries.

> "False forms compliment natural by imitating them, even representing false nipples as showing through the dress—'society ladies' often making love, as General Jackson fought, 'behind cotton breast works;' yet they are a shabby substitute, for they never vibrate; whereas natural ones quiver most bewitchingly at every step."

You might think our Mr. Fowler is verging on the lecherous, but shame on your false modesty. We should consider ourselves lucky to be the recipients of such straight talk from one who obviously has studied the subject so very closely.

And for that matter, thank you, Mr. Fowler, for bringing up the nipple. The nipples, if you did not know, are the semaphore flags of the womb. Says Fowler,

> "A girl whose bosom and nipples have just begun to form, catches a hard cold, which strikes to and palsies her womb, and stops its growth, and thereby their's. All nipple states tell all womb states, the nipples being larger or smaller as womb is either; they standing right out distinctly when it is well organized, and flat and imperfect when it is poor; their surrounding color bright red when it is rigorous and healthy, pale when it is dormant, and brownish, or yellowish, or darkish."

In other words, if a gentleman requests a nipple inspection before undertaking a marriage contract, you must understand where he is coming from. If you refuse him access to this important information, don't be surprised if he suspects you of trying to conceal a bilious womb and takes his leave of you.

Corpse's Curls and Sultry Scalp Grease

On to your crowning glory! As a nineteenth-century lady you have most likely let your hair grow unimpeded from childhood, a trend that will not change until the 1920s. Management of that mane is one more way the world judges your femininity. If you can't arrange a modest but fetching topknot, you probably can't breed robust sons either.

Have you ever seen an old-fashioned hairbrush, bristles no rougher than the back of a miffed cat, and wondered what in the world the point of it was? It could not possibly have tamed or styled hair. All it could

have been good for was patting your own head in congratulations after a particularly successful mammarial-balm session.

The truth is those brushes weren't meant to fight tangles or arrange hair in complex designs. For that you'll need your hard bone, wood, or ivory comb, with a possible touch of pomade, a hair-taming grease used by both sexes. Careful braiding is used to prevent snags, and as for styling, tread lightly, *ma petite.* A pleasing practical upsweep is about two twists and a curl away from simply wearing a hat that advertises your hourly rate.

The actual hairbrush's job here is twofold. One, to clean the day's soot and dirt from your hair at bedtime, because the nineteenth century is filthy. Second, to take the natural grease that your twenty-first-century self shampooed away every day, and distribute it down, down, down, all the way through your long and lusty Victorian mane. Grease is good when your hair is long enough to absorb it all; it provides luster and softness. You might as well tell yourself that, anyway, since washing your hair in the nineteenth century is a rare ordeal.

As for complex hair designs, Victorian ladies experiment with different fancy twists, and they play a bit with their "fringes" (bangs) throughout the century, but mostly you keep that business knotted up tight. And if you *are* one of those flighty little ninnies who chase fad and fashion, you'll likely need a bit of "false hair" to help you, i.e., hairpieces made from other women's locks, affixed to metal frameworks and then stuck into your own updo. Voilà, instant curls, volume,

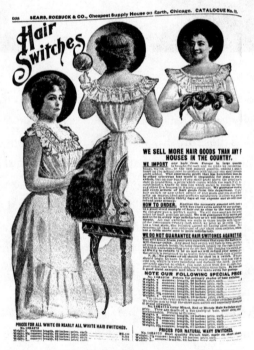

*Donor guaranteed to have survived at least
a fortnight after harvesting*

and chignon. The doomsayer Ellington warns that if you must indulge, for heaven's sake find a reputable hair dealer. The better the class of dealer, the more likely your hairpiece came off a diseased or starving but mostly alive European peasant girl, rather than her corpse.

Cosmetics:
You Might Want to Wait Another Half-Century

In the 1920s, a fellow named Max Factor developed an extremely well-made cosmetic foundation, which he called Pan-cake Makeup. He used it on the movie stars he worked with, so it had to be not only eye-pleasing and smooth (even hand-cranked film cameras were great at catching blemishes) but durable enough not to melt under the hot lights of early filmmaking. The rest is history. Mr. Factor and his knack for cosmetic chemistry are the reasons your grandma could touch up her eyes and lips before church without being treated like Mary Magdalene. Quality makeup is subtle and succeeds in the ultimate goal of making it hard to tell if you're actually wearing any.

But here we are, many, many years before Mr. Factor. *Your* makeup is terrible. In catalogs here it is usually listed with the pharmaceuticals or located somewhere between the toothpastes and the dog cleaners. An 1890s Montgomery Ward catalog displays two different brands of "cosmetique" (then as now, French names were used to add mystery to products that had no right to claim any) in three shades: black, pink, and white, which you can blend (somehow?) to create all the different touch-up colors your face needs. In consistency this stuff is similar to extremely greasy, heavy lipstick.

I don't recommend eyeliner, dear, though it is available in both pencil and paint form, often made from the same stuff as writing ink.

I'm simply saying it is near impossible to apply delicately and you'll look like an ancient Egyptian tart. But if you're determined, you might as well use all the tricks. It has also long been popular to squirt poison belladonna (deadly nightshade) in the eye. The poison dilates the pupil, giving, according to Ellington, "the upper part of the face a languishing, half-sentimental, half-sensual look." I imagine that look is probably born of confusion as to why the room has suddenly become so shiny, blurry, and poisonous. *"Why is it so bright in here?* I don't feel good. *Kiss me!"* Some catalogs explicitly say their cosmetics are intended only for the use of thespians, in much the same way modern medical marijuana is dispensed only for the treatment of glaucoma.

Lead: Good Enough for the *Mona Lisa,* Good Enough for You

You might know that lead, an ingredient used in certain paints and enamels even in the twenty-first century, is poisonous to the human body. That if you are repeatedly exposed to it, either through touch or inhalation, the lead accrues in your blood and tissue, causing nerve damage and death. But did you also know that it leaves the skin with a silky, fine finish when applied in white powder form?

White lead was the popular base of many early cosmetics, long before the nineteenth century. It often traveled under less terrifying names, like sugar of lead or Goulard's Extract. It was especially prevalent in a process called enameling that was all the rage in the late 1800s. A professional face enameler would remove all possible hair, dirt, and imperfections from his client's visage and then spread a shiny paste of white lead all over the face, neck, and bust. The result would be rejuvenated, smooth skin whose pores were clogged with both a youthful

SECRET OF A BEAUTIFUL FACE.

Every lady desires to be considered handsome. The most important adjunct to beauty is a clear, smooth, soft and beautiful skin. With this essential a lady appears handsome even if her features are not perfect.

Ladies afflicted with Tan, Freckles, Rough or Discolored Skin, should loose no time in procuring and applying

LAIRD'S
BLOOM OF YOUTH

It will immediately obliterate all such imperfections, and is entirely harmless. It has been chemically analyzed by the Board of Health of New York City, and pronounced entirely free from any material injurious to the health or skin.

Over two million ladies have used this delightful toilet preparation, and in every instance it has given entire satisfaction. Ladies, if you desire to be beautiful, give LAIRD'S BLOOM OF YOUTH a trial, and be convinced of its beautiful efficacy.

Seventy-Five Cents
per Bottle.

Sold by Fancy Goods Dealers and Druggists Everywhere.

Contains lead? Mayhap it does, mayhap it don't. I mean,
what exactly constitutes "injurious," anyway?

vivacity and a lethal mineral imbalance. Some sources say the process needed to be repeated a few times a week for true rejuvenation; others say a talented enameler could give you a pasting that would last up to five years, provided you weren't totally married to the idea of washing your face every day...or month.

Laird's Bloom of Youth was one such popular enamel. It contained a great deal of lead and was accused of causing a lead-poisoning palsy in its users. Immediately upon this report, around 1870, the makers of Laird's switched its main ingredient from lead to zinc and began protesting how safe the product was and how cruel the specious rumors of its lead content had been.

Even at the height of its popularity, some people found lead enameling repugnant. An 1872 edition of the *Sacramento Daily Union* gave a gossipy account of the horrors encountered by two uppity society ladies who thought they could cheat time through chemistry. Oh, but they got what was a'coming to them.

"A lady in Louisville paid $75, we are told, for having her face enameled for the ball given at the Gait House to the Grand Duke Alexis. The enamel was warranted to last three days, and so it did. The lady was taken ill upon her return home from the ball, her face became greatly swollen, the most acute pain succeeded, and it was only by the employment of the best medical aid that her life was saved. This statement we have from an undoubted source.

But the case of this lady is not so bad as that of another Louisville lady who became enamored of the odious fashion of enameling the face[. She] visited another city, far to the eastward, some five months ago, for the sole purpose of having her face enameled according to the latest Parisian mode. She had heard that a noted Parisian was engaged in the enameling business at the city in question, and to him she went upon her arrival. For the sum of $500 he agreed to enamel her face so scientifically that the enamel would remain undamaged for three years, and a year or two longer if extra care was taken in washing the face according to his prescribed method....The lady received the enamel and returned to this city. Since her return she has disappeared from society. There was so much poison in the enamel that its effects were almost total paralysis of the facial nerves, and what was once a beautiful face is now a distorted and ulcerous one."

Keep in mind, there were no celebrity tabloids back then, and they didn't have the catharsis of watching Hollywood housewives crash and burn. Something had to fill the void. So we must forgive the author if she takes a very obvious joy in the necrotized flesh of fellow females.

Of course, people knew lead wasn't entirely safe, and soon they declared it decidedly *unsafe*. That wasn't an opinion shared by everyone. The author of an 1869 book sternly titled *Toilet Secrets*, known only as Incognita, is quite tired of hearing about how bad lead is for you.

Says Incognita,

> "Now, a few words about this said 'poisoning.'…The practice of crying down everything, wholesale, in the way of 'lead,' is just as absurd as if a teetotal lecture is to convince a moderate man he is going headlong to destruction and drunkenness, because he takes his sherry and port, like an Englishman should take it, and like every sensible medical man recommends it."

Oh, a smidgen of lead rubbed into your sore eyes on occasion can't be that bad. Incognita is willing to stake her name and reputation on—oh. Well. Let's move on.

Skin Care: Fire Cleanses All

Freckles aren't cute in this era. They're deformities that cry out to the world, "I'm a slack-jawed, unrefined girl who stands in the sun all day with m'cows and m'corn and I don't know the difference between a soirée and a sodee pop." So we'll need to scorch those right off. Many of the lady writers suggest variations of lemon juice, which is still recommended today as a safe way to temporarily fade freckles. But Thomas S. Sozinskey, in his 1877 *Personal Appearance and the Culture of Beauty, with Hints as to Character,* cuts right through that namby-pamby nonsense.

Don't scorn a creature such as this! They deserve only pity! They too are humans, underneath their deformities.

"Unquestionably the best way of getting rid of them or any other discoloration, when very bad, is to eat them out with muriatic [carbolic] acid slightly diluted, or by applying a blister, or by exposing the face to the sun until it becomes burned sufficiently to be followed by exfoliation of the skin. This last is an excellent remedy and it takes only a few days to effect a cure."

Granted, the freckles will return because they inhabit a dermal layer deeper than the one you just painfully removed with extreme amounts of ultraviolet radiation. But take heart, so will the sun return! And you can just keep sloughing off layers of your face for however many years it takes to develop either the skin cancer, or the common sense, to slow you down.

You'll find similar treatments, both prepackaged and home-prepared, for pimples and blackheads (once thought to be facial worms, since squeezing the clogged pore resulted in the excavation of a worm-like deposit). But frankly, if you're going to be aggressive about these deformities you might as well head straight for the arsenic.

Yes, Dr. Campbell's "safe arsenic complexion wafers" are among the more deadly poisons known to man, but we can't make a pure-complexion omelet without breaking a few cerebrovascular eggs.

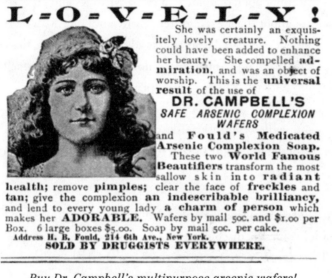

L ∙O∙ V∙ E ∙L∙ Y !

She was certainly an exquisitely lovely creature. Nothing could have been added to enhance her beauty. She compelled **admiration**, and was an object of worship. This is the **universal result** of the use of

DR. CAMPBELL'S
SAFE ARSENIC COMPLEXION WAFERS

and **Fould's Medicated Arsenic Complexion Soap.** These two **World Famous Beautifiers** transform the most sallow skin into **radiant health**; remove **pimples**; clear the face of **freckles** and **tan**; give the complexion **an indescribable brilliancy,** and lend to every young lady **a charm of person** which makes her **ADORABLE.** Wafers by mail 50c. and $1.00 per Box. 6 large boxes $5.00. Soap by mail 50c. per cake. Address H. B. Fould, 214 6th Ave., New York. **SOLD BY DRUGGISTS EVERYWHERE.**

Buy Dr. Campbell's multipurpose arsenic wafers! Stellar skin treatment and a reliable rat poison!

Wrinkles

Oh, gracious. All this information is taxing you, isn't it? I see that you're frowning, trying to process it all. This is why no physician worth his two-year apprenticeship at sea will encourage heavy thought to trample through a female brain. Darling, your frown is causing wrinkles! *Wrinkles!*

A woman's face is her introduction to the world, and wrinkles force her to present a shabby and worn calling card! Where do wrinkles come from? Why do they occur? Well, as you might expect, wrinkles are the result of all the things you're doing wrong.

Do you favor a side when you sleep? According to *Beauty: Its Attainment and Preservation,* published in 1892,

"Sleeping upon one side will cause wrinkles and crow's-feet to form about the eyes, and frequently more lines will be seen around one eye than the other. It is advisable, therefore, to sleep upon the back if possible, and if not, to accustom one's-self to sleeping alternately upon both sides."

Do you wallow in misery like a sow in slop? Because, as Shoemaker, he of the pineapple breast, reminds us, that is another primary cause of wrinkles.

"A great many people worry themselves into ugliness and foster it by nursing discontent. Keep the blood warm and the well filled with affection and there is no danger of the face shriveling."

Of course all of that is for naught if you happen to live in one of those putrid wastelands known as cities. Says Shoemaker,

"City people are more afflicted with wrinkles than country people are, and the reason is simply because the conditions necessary to happiness are not as good in the city as in the country."

To remove these etchings of personal misery and poor sleeping habits, a surprising number of beauty counselors recommend tying meat to your face. Says Lady Montez,

"I knew many fashionable ladies in Paris who used to bind their faces, every night on going to bed, with thin slices of raw beef, which is said to keep the skin from wrinkles, while it gives a youthful freshness and brilliancy to the complexion. I have no doubt of its efficacy."

Mud house, window, and what might one day be a tree.
A sweet country life of ease, not a wrinkle in sight.

These "sleep with something perishable on your face" cures usually involve trying to replace lost fatty tissue, to plump up that which has wrinkled. Various substitutes for your own face fat included: sheep's wool soaked in sheep's fat, olive oil, almond oil, beeswax, spermaceti (don't worry, not what it sounds like; it's just a gooey waxy substance created inside a sperm whale's head that early whalers thought *looked* like semen), veal, and lard. Late-century catalogs pioneered serial-killer style rubber masks to help keep whatever spoiling food you hoped would turn back the clock tightly affixed to your face.

There, now. We've got you clean, menstruating

with charm, and able to keep your face, hair, and body just as pleasant as sperm whale by-products and unfairly villainized poisons will permit. It is time to go forth armed with your new knowledge, *ma petite,* and begin the hunt.

7

Courtship:
Not-Talking Your Way into His Heart

*T*ake your umbrella out of your mouth. Sucking the handle of one's parasol is apparently a common practice among young ladies, either as a nervous habit or a dreadfully misguided attempt to display the possibilities of a sensual mouth. It's not as beguiling as you think and will not help you find a husband of character. Mrs. Florence Hartley, in her 1872 *The Ladies' Book of Etiquette, and Manual of Politeness: A Complete Handbook for the Use of the Lady in Polite Society*, addressed the issue most succinctly:

> "What are you doing? Sucking the head of your parasol! Have you not breakfasted? Take that piece of ivory from your mouth! To suck it is unlady-like, and let me tell you, excessively unbecoming. Rosy lips and pearly teeth can be put to a better use."

Now that we have *that* settled, we can address the finer points of making yourself man-worthy.

George Napheys was one of the first to write approachable, non-pornographic literature on the subjects of sex and hygiene. And for this we will give him due credit, no matter how queerly his words fall upon our modern ears. *The Physical Life of Woman: Advice to the Maiden, Wife and Mother,* which Napheys began writing in 1869, devotes much attention to that golden time betwixt maidenhood and wifehood: the courtship.

Give Him NOTHING

You are a prize to be won. He must work to capture your affections and approval. Only the stupid and slutty trout leap out of the water to gain the fisherman's attention. The virtuous trout simply allows the sun to gleam briefly on her shining scales and then dives back to the shadowy depths. Only a skilled man with the finest of fake bugs can ream a metal hook through *her* mouth. You are that trout, and the metal hook you are about to be impaled on is holy matrimony. Napheys explains:

"A wise provision of nature ordains that woman shall be sought. She flees, and man pursues. The folly of modern reformers, who would annul this provision, is evident. Were it done away with, man, ever prone to yield to woman's solicitations, and then most prone when yielding is most dangerous, would fritter away his powers at an early

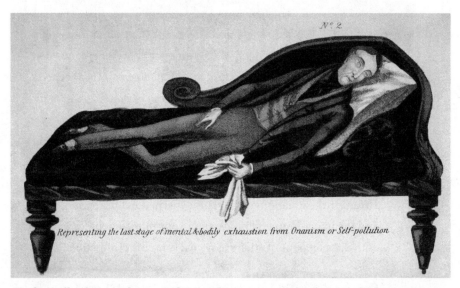

Representing the last stage of mental & bodily exhaustion from Onanism or Self-pollution

Technically this gentleman is languishing as a result of masturbation, not sexual indulgence. But the perilous loss of vital fluids is the same in either case.

age, and those very impulses which nature has given to perpetuate the race would bring about its destruction."

That is to say, if there were ever to come a time when women cast off the tradition of modest reluctance and approached men romantically, the epic loss of semen due to man's endless acquiescence would sap not only his strength, but his ability to propagate the human race. This fact is reinforced by my other favorite authors in this genre, Benjamin Grant Jefferis and J. L. Nichols, who wrote the tremendously popular *Search Lights on Health: Light on Dark Corners—A Complete Sexual Science and a Guide to Purity and Physical Manhood* in 1895. They agree. Flirting is just murder on your testicles.

J. L. Nichols is not a trifler.

"The young man who may take pleasure in the fact that he is the hero of half a dozen or more engagements and love episodes, little realizes that such constant excitement often causes not only dangerously frequent and long-continued nocturnal emissions, but most painful affections of the testicles. Those who show too great familiarity with the other sex, who entertain lascivious thoughts, continually exciting the sexual desires, always suffer a weakening of power and sometimes the actual diseases of degeneration, chronic inflammation of the gland, spermatorrhoea, impotence, and the like.—Young man, beware; your punishment for trifling with the affections of others may cost you a life of affliction."

See, men can trifle with their excretions, too! But men are weak when it comes to sexual restraint. Which is why, my angel, it is so very,

very important that women be ashamed of their bodies. And their desires. Let's just say everything. Question every facet of yourself as a human, constantly, just to be safe. After all, only *your* self-loathing can keep the human race thriving. Says Napheys,

> "To prevent such a disaster, woman is endowed with a sense of shame, an invincible modesty, her greatest protection, and her greatest charm. Let her never forget it, never disregard it; for without it she becomes the scorn of her own sex and the jest of the other."

Fumbled Flirtings

Of course this would suggest a woman is powerless, unable to grease the cogs of love in her own favor by word or deed! Fie, darling. Women are much too wily for that. If you choose, you may engage in the delicate art of flirting. And I mean *delicate*. Nothing so crass as winking,

The sexual tension is almost unbearable.

saying hello, or smiling. You don't want him to think you're easy. No, Victorians had a whole language of love that is largely lost to us today: that of flirting through your fashion accessories.

It's a very complex language with, in my opinion, much room for misinterpretation. Below are some examples of object flirtation, as sampled from 1890's *The Mystery of Love, Courtship and Marriage Explained*, by Henry J. Wehman. I have included each action's intended secret meaning and what it probably actually meant whenever it occurred. Get that parasol out of your mouth, dear, you're going to need it.

HANDKERCHIEF FLIRTATIONS

Dropping it in front of a man

Intended: "We can be friends!"

Actual: "Wow. I cannot believe I'm supposed to carry my own snot around with me all day. So disgusting. Ugh…maybe I can…just drop it? Just pretend I lost it?"

Twirling it in both hands

Intended: "I am indifferent to you."

Actual: "Bored. So bored. Church lasts three hours in this century? Heh, hey, look! I can twirl to the beat of 'We Will Rock You' and no one even knows I'm doing it."

Drawing it across the cheek

Intended: "I love you."

Actual: "Agh! That was the third bug to splatter on my face! Stupid open carriages! Staring at a horse's pooper for hours while my internal organs get knocked out of place with every bone-shattering bump. How is this romantic?"

FAN FLIRTATIONS

Carrying it in your left hand

Intended: "I desire your acquaintance."

Actual: "I am left-handed. But I'm not supposed to be. Don't tell people."

Placing it on the right ear

Intended: "You have changed."

Actual: "Oh, holy cow. Oh, man. I am itching like crazy. I really need to have Mother go over my scalp for nits again. She's gonna have to come up with something better than soaking my head in onion juice and boric acid because I am *not* doing that again."

Drawing it across the forehead

Intended: "We are watched!"

Actual: "Really freakin' hot in here. Oh, yeah, I carry a fan now. Whew!"

PARASOL FLIRTATIONS

Striking it on your hand

Intended: "I am very much displeased!"

Actual: "You told everyone I was left-handed? Mister, this is my special smackin' umbrella, and I am going to wallop you so hard your great-great-grandchildren will feel it and have to pay a really high bill for an MRI that won't show anything, because it doesn't pick up on time-travel whuppins. So step off!"

Folding it

Intended: "Get rid of your friends!"

Actual: "Why did I bring this? It's England. The sun never even shines!"

Dropping it
Intended: "I love you."

Actual: "Darn. That must be a parasol for right-handed people."

"For the last time, I stumbled on my dress and I just dropped *it. It doesn't mean we're eloping tonight! Now shove off!"*

GLOVE FLIRTATIONS

Biting the tips of the fingers
Intended: "I wish to be rid of you very soon."

Actual: "Go away so I can suck my parasol. Oh, I can just taste it."

Turning them inside out
Intended: "I hate you."

Actual: "This stitching is atrocious. Seriously, if I order something *bespoke* I expect the clothier to hire peasants with nimble fingers."

Dropping them
Intended: "I love you."

Actual: "Argh! Trip on one beggar child, and there goes a new pair of hand-sewn white deerskin leather matinee-length gloves that cost like eighty dollars in real money. Right into a pile of horse manure. I HATE THIS CENTURY."

Shame: The Sweetest Blessing

Disingenuous and perplexing? Not something you'd want to try? Good.

Because it was a test, my girl! Only harlots do something as base as *flirt*. I mean, really, darling. Perhaps we should save time, dispense with the gloves and fans altogether. You could just back your rump up and present for him like an alley cat in heat! No flirting! You are a *lady*. Jefferis and Nichols explain how the character of the flirting woman is desperately lacking in shame.

Flirting and Its Dangers.

HOW MANY YOUNG GIRLS ARE RUINED.

> "Who is the flirt…in the streets after dark, boisterous and noisy in their conversation, gossiping and giggling, flirting with first one and then another, will soon settle their matrimonial prospects among good society. Modesty is a priceless jewel. No sensible young man with a future will marry a flirt."

Men don't find an outward display of joy appealing! "Joy" doesn't get the roast on the table by 6 p.m. sharp! Chitchat doesn't help a woman survive having nine babies! Flirtation leads to familiarity, a state of being that has wrenching consequences, as explained in Melville C. Keith's 1890 *The Young Lady's Private Counselor: The Care of Mind and Body; A Book Designed for Young Ladies, to Aid Them in Acquiring a Life of Purity, Intellectual Culture, Bodily Strength and Freedom from Many of the Ills and Annoyances of Life That Custom Has Placed on the Sex* (yes, that is the title— TYLPCTCMBBDYLATALPICBSFMIALCHPS for short):

"Undue familiarity cheapens a girl even in her lover's eyes and lays the foundation of future jealousy and possible murder. There is plenty of time for familiarity after marriage."

Our author does not diagram the transition from flirting to homicide. But does he really need to? I mean, who doesn't look at a teenager fluttering her eyelashes at some boy and think, "That's going to end with three corpses in a filthy, blood-soaked basement"? And let's not forget that flirting is a gateway to more serious and life-ruining forms of canoodling. Tell us more, Messrs. Jefferis and Nichols:

Canoodlers! Canoodlers, by God!

"Kissing, Fondling, and Caressing Between Lovers.—This should never be tolerated under any circumstances, unless there is an engagement to justify it, and then only in a sensible and limited way. The girl who allows a young man the privilege of kissing her or putting his arms around her waist before engagement will at once fall in the estimation of the man she has thus gratified and desired to please."

That is what happens when you ignore your God-given sense of shame, lambkin. He wants to put his arm around your waist. You bashfully allow him to. He realizes you're a dirty slut and wants nothing more to do with you. A + B = C, and C = you dying alone with syphilis. Simple math to complement the rather creative science we've been citing, such as "The purity of woman is doubly attrac-

"Lydia! Is that a letter from another beau? Oh, you know how cross that makes me! I'm going to go get my dueling cravat."

tive, and sensuality in her becomes doubly offensive and repellent. It is contrary to the laws of nature for a man to love a harlot" (Jefferis and Nichols).

Just look at it from his perspective: "If she lets me put *my* arm around her waist, how many other arms have been there before mine? When I'm hugging her, I'm hugging every person she has ever hugged. Even worse, she appears to enjoy this warm romantic touch. That isn't natural! It means her brain is addlepated (likely from too much masturbation) into a simmering state of pre-hysteria. She's a time bomb. A hussy time bomb!"

That is what your intended will be thinking as he hurries away from your poisoned touch. If he be wise, that is. If he is the sort who does not care about the vitality of his testicles, he may stay. But that's not the sort of man you want for a husband, is it?

*Content, even sensuous-looking, isn't she? Her photo is part of a
series documenting women who've been institutionalized for Hysteria.
And that, darling, is why we don't smile in the streets.*

Of course, as a woman, there are some physical reactions you can't
help engaging in when you are in love. Just ask our dear Mr. Fowler.

"All women with a loved man always thus set their breasts forward
towards him, and so that if in low dress, they would exhibit the upper
part of their bosoms. Beaux, this sign tells you infallibly that your girl
loves you, and its absence that she does not."

Oh, it may be inconvenient, you enjoying a chat with your mother
only to be struck into silence when *zing!* Your beloved enters the room
and your breasts snap to attention like good soldiers saluting their
commanding officer. But true love is hard work, darling.

Eugenics—Not Just for Nazis

So how *does* one go about securing lifelong love without compromising virtue? Luckily Jefferis and Nichols gave that quite a bit of thought. Now, be open-minded and try not to think of Hitler.

That may be directly where your brain goes when you hear the word "eugenics." But eugenics is about more than a moving wall of blond, blue-eyed Teutons goose-stepping in perfect formation across Europe. The idea itself is fascinating, and it's the basic process used in agriculture and animal husbandry: the fastest mare is locked in a stable with the strongest stud with the hopes that their vicious and horrifying love will produce a Kentucky Derby champion. Our turkeys are huge-breasted and our tomatoes transport well with minimum spoilage because of selective breeding.

So *what if,* thought many a Victorian thinker with too much time on his hands, we did that with humans? Wouldn't that be marvelous? Strong people with balanced mentality would reproduce, and we could sterilize the weak, unintelligent, and sickly, or just forbid them to marry, and wait for the dregs of humanity to slowly die off. Could anything be more natural?

Margaret Sanger, the visionary founder of Planned Parenthood who broke many laws in her efforts to give women the right to control how often they get pregnant, believed in eugenics, which troubles many who want to lionize her today. But lots of intelligent people believed in eugenics. They weren't all evil, and they weren't necessarily trying to breed a master race. Some of them just thought eugenics could help stem the endless tide of poverty, illness, and starvation that saturated the nineteenth century. They saw it as a way to stop a lot of suffering before it started.

It was also incredibly draconian and impossible to implement without violating basic human rights. But we're talking about an era when constantly drunk men labored in coal mines fourteen hours a day and took their eleven-year-old wives to watch a mentally disabled man accused of horse theft be executed in the center of town as a special treat. It was not a gentle time. Human rights was an idea brewing, but it brewed over a very low heat.

Selecting the Right Head Lumps

Young ladies, indelibly fix this shape of head in your memories. Any man who will make a natural, kind and true husband will have a head in outline from a side view like this.

I just wanted you to have a good grasp of the importance of eugenics and selective breeding when you read Jefferis and Nichols's advice on selecting a mate. They sound—they sound a tad severe, I know. But hear them out.

First, you must select your future husband scientifically.

"If you court at all, court scientifically. Bungle whatever else you will, but do not bungle courtship. A failure in this may mean more than a loss of wealth or public honors; it may mean ruin, or a life often worse than death. The world is full of wretched and mis-mated people."

This of course meant that hot-tempered women should marry coolheaded men and shy ladies fit well with glad-handers. Jefferis and Nichols even extended this theory to body builds. Stout should marry slender, short should marry tall, and so forth.

A scientifically perfect match

"Bright red hair should marry jet black, and jet black, auburn or bright red, etc. And the more red-faced and bearded or impulsive a man, the more dark, calm, cool and quiet should his wife be; and vice versa. The florid should not marry the florid, but those who are dark, in proportion they themselves are light. Red-whiskered men should marry brunettes, but no blondes; the color of the whiskers being more determinate of the temperament than that of the hair."

This is fact. Hair color and complexion tones precisely indicate your personality. They just do. No! Stop right there. It's the nineteenth century and you're a woman; I owe you no explanation. Hush, now, men are trying to teach you something that might one day save you from a murder-suicide pact.

Phrenology allows you to tell whether a man will make a terrible husband just by asking him to remove his hat. Here's a tip from Jefferis and Nichols: "Do Not Marry a Man With a Low, Flat Head; for, however fascinating, genteel, polite, tender, plausible or winning he may be, you will repent the day of your espousal."

Conversely, there are appearances *you* want to avoid presenting so that you may attract the finest-quality husband. You serve many purposes as a wife, but the most important is incubating and extruding his biological legacy from your body. You'd better look like you're up for the task. We've already covered man's attraction to full bosoms, youth, and healthy-hued skin. But there is more to consider. When it comes to a woman's possible deficiencies in pleasing a husband, there is *always* more to consider. Take it from Jefferis and Nichols:

"Wasp Waists.—Marrying small waists is attended with consequences scarcely less disastrous than marrying rich and fashionable girls. An amply developed chest is a sure indication of a naturally vigorous constitution and a strong hold on life; while small waists indicate small and feeble vital organs, a delicate constitution, sickly offspring and a short life. Beware of them, therefore, unless you wish your heart broken by the early death of your wife and children."

Note the practicality. Our authors don't question the virtue or amiability of the potential bride; they simply advise, in true eugenic fashion, that she is improper breeding stock and therefore should gracefully remove herself from marital considerations and live a sweet, short life all alone, or maybe with some friends who also have teeny organs, and not pass the burden of her weakness on to children.

"Mrs. Pancakes and I have teeny organs. We didn't wanna fall in love and have kittens anyway, did we, Mrs. Pancakes?"

Love just isn't in the cards for everyone, dear. If God wanted you to have a husband He'd have given you thick, sturdy thighs and wide-set birthing hips.

Love Is Blind, But Everyone Else Is Watching

Here you are. Although your physique and social class suggest your perfect scientific match is to be found within the limp embrace of an anemic Englishman in silk breeches, your heart rebels. Perhaps you're drawn instead to the damp brow of a hardworking freedman fighting all odds to build the life of his dreams. Or perhaps you are an elder lady, who has overripened past the age of twenty-five, and you are drawn to the kind eyes of a widowed Chinese landlord who wants nothing more than to adorn you in jasmine-scented robes and opium tinctures. (I do not judge; that actually sounds like a lovely retirement plan.)

We know that you can marry your first cousin, of course, as Her Majesty the Queen has done. You can marry a man whose parents came from a different Western European country. (Not Irish or Italian, obviously; they're a very colorful people best left to themselves. But the Swedes and Prussians are wholesome, sturdy folk.) You can even marry a man thirty years your senior, providing he remains active enough to keep his spermatozoa hopping!

But can you marry outside of your own race?

Oh, bless your heart. Your stupid, stupid heart.

Using the wrong *fork* can cause weeks of gossip. Calling a person you've known your whole life by their Christian name is coarse and improper. Unless you're a grizzled French-Canadian fur trapper who takes a widowed squaw into his shack in exchange for three beaver pelts, the answer is no.

Napheys prides himself on dealing with hard truths that other Victorian writers are too timid to approach. Here he interprets the shocking situation of interracial marriage through the lens of pure science that he heard from a guy.

> "It is well known that the black race cannot survive a northern climate. Dr. Snow, of Providence, Rhode Island, who has given great attention to the study of statistics, says emphatically that, in New England, the colored population inevitably perish in a few generations, if left to themselves. This debility no woman should wish to give to her children."

I don't know what "inevitably perish" means, I'll admit. But that must be why no black people ever lived in wintry places like Chicago or New Yo—wait a minute. Huh.

That is but one reason of many Napheys and every other writer of the era give for why color lines should not be crossed. You do not want to hear the others. To be sure, there were interracial marriages nonetheless, especially in the undeveloped western United States. But rarely among the class of people who owned oyster forks. The Victorian era provided the foundation for social change, with the end of slavery and the beginning of suffrage and other civil rights movements. But just the foundation.

Spinsterhood

Now, there is the remote possibility that you did not come here for the muttonchops. Perhaps you'd rather not fuss with the whole mess that men bring into your life. If that be true, you, my friend, are heading for what is called spinsterhood. It is the female equivalent of "bachelor," except it's not sexy or fun and everyone secretly despises you although they'd be hard pressed to say exactly why. Because after all, spinsters are historically valuable members of society, according to a particular old maid identifying only as Pearl in an 1895 issue of *The Monthly Packet:*

> "The old-fashioned suppressed spinster of our own youth… was called upon, before the days of trained nurses, to help in illness in other people's houses; not only brothers and sisters, but first, and even second, cousins, claimed her services at births and deaths. She was as much excited by a love affair in any family with

"Having a high time, not a man in sight!" That's right, dearie. Stay positive. Your plank and barrel are just lovely.

which she was intimate as the family itself, and was nearly always asked to weddings and christenings. Her life was full of reflected interest, and she took her share in the world, as one may say, by proxy."

Pearl goes on to lament the "modern" spinster, who looks down on the simple wife and mother and who insists that any woman who doesn't want to talk about cats and suffrage is a dullard. What happened to the sweet spinster of old, who was exquisitely happy to watch as every woman in the family fell in love and went out to live her life while she sated her passion sketching ferns? The old girl whom you could rely on to come nurse your family through highly contagious diseases, since—not to be callous, but—God forbid she fall ill, it's not like she had a *great deal* to live for in the first place.

We must again rely on Mr. Fowler to give us the real story on spinsterhood. It was a sickness, affecting uppity women. And they suffered for their arrogance. Simply put, without a man in your life, you're already dead inside.

> "You have no fond partner with whom to while away life's now tedious days and nights, in pleasant talks, walks, rides and visits, on whom to lean, with whom to live; nor any rosy children to love, amuse, wait on, and nurse you; but are like a barren trailing vine, instead of clinging to some sturdy oak loaded with fruit; living a dreary life, and awaiting a drearier death."

I know, it's harsh. But honestly, darling, everyone is already thinking it. Here in the nineteenth century you won't even get the courtesy of people wondering if you are a lesbian. They just assume you are excruciatingly undesirable. To put it in modern terms, an absolute dumpster fire.

It's wonderful if you are young and pretty and can afford to be picky. But if you yourself are lumpy and obnoxious, you might have to disregard all the careful laws of choosing a good husband and settle down with the first flat-headed, foul-breathed rapscallion miscreant who gooses your bustle. But if that's starting to look like the only option, my girl, you grab the ticket and ride that train straight to Perdition.

The reason this man is an unreliable husband is because he is very weak in Conjugality and Parental Love and exceedingly strong in Amativeness. Young ladies, beware of such men as husbands.

"Old maids, think back how 'love cracked' some one of your admirers obviously once

Good. Enough. For you.

was. You should have improved that precious season. You went farther and fared worse, and now wish you had accepted what you could then have obtained."

Yes, dear, let Brother Fowler's violent poetry wash over you; don't fight it. It's so much easier to accept your feminine role in this world if you don't struggle.

"Your punishment must increase with years. You may stifle first love, and get along passably till thirty, when Nature revolts and chastises. Life becomes objectless or else distracted, or like a corn, perpetually aching. Enduring love's crucifixion long withers or crushes out. Age widens your loveless gulf. Society gives you no right to love, nor be caressed, not even to reciprocate friendship, but shuts you in and out from men. Your age-marks belie your assumed youth. Your bloom withers and perishes."

Just you, your useless corn life, and a society that thinks your portion of the town's oxygen could be better used to ignite a drunk's flatulence for a good laugh at the alehouse.

Find a man, *cherie*. And quick. Bring forth the wedding bells.

8

The Wedding Night, or:
A Bad Bit of Bumbo

The reluctant bride

*T*he goal in Victorian fiction is marriage. Well, unless the goal is to solve a murder in a Rue Morgue or safely navigate the Mississippi on a raft. Otherwise, we look to the stories set in and written during the 1800s for particular, pristine love. That breathless moment when couples finally overcome the obstacles that society has placed in their paths and are united forever. Usually those obstacles existed only because rules of delicacy forbade the characters from speaking truths.

A whole novel can be based on the fact that a girl won't or can't say that she'd rather *not* have to marry her homosexual cousin, nor the beastly estate owner whose water rights her scheming brother wants to secure, nor even the sixty-three-year-old ex-quartermaster who saved her father's life by pilfering him extra leeches to drain his dangerous surfeit of blood while they were fighting the Boers in the Battle of Boomplaats. Types of conflict were limited in Victorian ladies' literature; it was either dramatic courtships, dying siblings, or the perils of harsh orphanages. The latter two having considerably less romantic potential.

So I certainly understand if you are approaching your marriage with near-deranged euphoria. You have been conditioned to do so. Unlike in the twenty-first century, where a happy marriage was meant to be treated as but one (optional) part of a healthy life, here it is the game-winning throw. This is the climax of your life.

The wedding? Well, the writers of nineteenth-century hygiene books usually insist on small home ceremonies with only family in attendance, no extravagances more expensive than crepe paper, the bride being married in sensible clothing she can wear again, and while you're at it, no honeymoon. It's bad for the bride's nerves.

But all these books are written by men. Most of whom, as a species, still wish they could command weddings to be carried out in this manner. The ladies' magazines of the era felt differently and laid great importance on bridesmaids' dresses and flower arrangements and even wedding photography, just as they do today. So enjoy the wedding. This is the one part of your journey you can re-create just as it was painted in your dreams, no bothersome bodily functions or inconvenient social mores to muck you up.

Those are going to start up again very promptly, however.

Welcome to your wedding night, lambkin.

Dreams really do come true, if you cinch your corset tight enough.

The Riddle of the Vagina

You, my time-traveling friend, know more than a virgin bride of Victoriana *should* know about making love. Truly, you know more than anybody here, due to your own century's advanced science and frank acceptance of human sexuality. It honestly doesn't matter your particulars. An eighty-three-year-old cloistered nun who has seen the male member only as it appears in paintings of the baby Jesus portrayed by the Italian masters of the High Renaissance *still* knows more than these folks do about a woman's sexuality. For man is fearfully and wonderfully made.

Women, mostly just fearfully.

Take the riddle of the vagina. Or as James Ashton put it in 1861's *The Book of Nature:*

"This curved tube [that] possesses some curious powers, which are in action only during connection with the male."

Medical Counsellings, by Robert James Culverwell (1841), attempts to further explain that curious power, by describing the miracle of life

in scientific terms. Unfortunately the science of 1841 doesn't exactly know what's going on during the miracle of life.

"The male is destined to furnish a peculiar fecundating secretion, and is accordingly provided with glands to prepare such fluid, and a conduit to convey the same to its proper destination; while the female, being the recipient, possesses an organ capable of effecting a mysterious yet specific change upon the fluid so deposited."

Culverwell,
fecundating his fluids

In layman's terms, a lady takes the "fecundating secretion" that is…conveyed…out of a man into her tube with peculiar powers. This fearsome excretion then finds its way to the female receptacle, an organ bag in her belly. And then we're not—we're not quite sure. The man's secretion turns into a baby. I imagine if God wanted us to know the particulars He wouldn't have buried the whole nasty business so

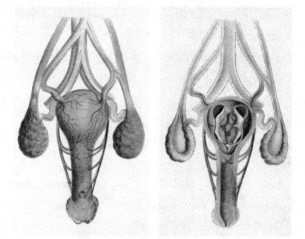

*The female reproductive system, helpfully laid out as if
it were the male reproductive system. Except for the tiny
embarrassed fetus in the middle.*

deep inside your guts, would He? And that is why nineteenth-century
parents tell their children that babies happen when an angel's laughter
falls into a cabbage patch and Papa buys it from the grocer. Because
the truth as they understand it isn't that much clearer, except that it has
penises in it and no one wants to hear about that.

How to Capture, Mount, Pin, and Preserve
the Northern Full-Breasted Virgin

Of course, dear one, you cannot let on the depth of your knowledge
about your magic tube, nor his fecund potion, nor what they are to do
in conjunction. A new bride is to face her wedding night with a completely symptomless sexuality, dormant inside you, to be awakened
only by your lawful husband's touch. So from here on out, let us have

you assume the full guise of this maiden bride, with all her charming ignorance and membranes intact.

The new you is described thusly in 1895's *The Doctor's Plain Talk to Young Men,* written by the impossibly perfectly named Dr. Virgil Primrose English:

> "[The bride] is not deficient in sexuality and amativeness; but her mind and habits have been so pure, and free from lust, that there has never been anything to produce an excitement of the sexual passions. She may be indifferent regarding intercourse, and she may look upon it with horror."

One could argue that it is possible, given perfect conditions, for a young girl to *not* fantasize about kisses and caresses as pubescent gears begin their aching grind. Especially if those conditions involved keeping the girl in a medically induced coma. One could also argue that no man in his right mind would believe a woman could reach maturity without sexual longings, only to have them surge to life fully inflamed upon her entering his specific bed. However, one shouldn't spend so much time "arguing" if she intends to keep a man. Shush.

Dr. Charles A. Hoff, who wrote *Highways and Byways to Health* in 1887, insists: a woman on her wedding night should be but "the fair creature who lies by his side wondering what fate has in store for her trembling modesty."

George W. Hudson's 1883 *The Marriage Guide for Young Men* actually offers one of the more thoughtful reasons, aside from physical pain, that a bride dreads this moment. He assumes she has no sexual cravings, of course. He wouldn't want to insult his male reader by suggesting his hypothetical bride would have been involved in the lewd activities that stir up such desires, such as riding horses astride or bathing with frequency. But psychologically she is giving up that last bit of power that gave her an equal footing with her husband.

> "It will be quite a shock to feminine modesty when she, a pure-minded maiden, shall be called upon to lie down in the same bed with a man. It will seem repulsive at first, because she will feel that lying down robs her of her feminine prerogative, and puts her person in the power of another. To some women the shock is painful; it matters not that those with whom they are to lie down, are their own lovers with whom they have passed so many pleasant hours; everything is new, and it takes them some time to fall in with the new order of things."

Up until now, your man has been doing everything in his power to convince you of his worth. He strove to earn your respect and affections. Perhaps you thought it was because he found you pleasing to look upon and pleasurable to talk to. You thought he daydreamed about watching you sing tender lullabies to your newborn babes, that he would pat his tummy while bragging to the boys at the shop about your Sunday roasts. And he probably is looking forward to those things.

But those aren't the reasons he's rearranged his whole life, quit himself of many a pleasurable bad habit, and worked hard for a promotion so he may take on the financial responsibility of your every need as well as whatever children he creates. That stuff, dear one, is a whole lot of trouble. There are few impulses in human nature strong enough to motivate a man to embrace that burden.

As Dr. Ashton, who is not a man to mince words, eloquently puts it:

"It is useless to deny that the majority of marriages which are apparently based on the sentiment called love, are nothing more than the result of an involuntary obedience to the imperious voice of our sexual organs."

As demonstrated by these late-nineteenth-century Chinese fertility figures. Except— probably not as happy.

The Featherbed Jig. Entering Convivial Society. Making Feet for Baby Stockings. Bit of Bumbo. To Be Found in Bread and Butter Fashion. Carvel's Ring. A Bit of the Fruitful Vine. To Join Giblets. Do Some Docking! Sex, dear. Even if love is only an illusion created by your vagina, he wants a piece of the dream.

Laying the Groundwork for a Lifetime of Suffering

Books on marital hygiene and happiness unanimously counseled a man to remember his manners on that first night. That though he was paying ever so dearly to possess her, his wife was his cherished bride, not some common drap bunter trumpery wrinkle-bellied hedge whore! (There is so much terrific slang available in this century. You can't use any of it, of course.) Says Hudson,

"You may think that you can then throw off all restraint, and make her feel that she is yours, but beware! though she will be yours, she will have her maidenly feelings...she will be the same

"No, everything's fine! She talked it over with her mother, and they decided ether was the best way to tackle the problem."

modest young lady whom you courted, but do not shock her modesty. Treat her with the same consideration as when you courted her."

There were reasons beyond common decency to treat your bride with patience and gentleness that first night. Most of the authors on the topic agreed that a poorly executed initial marital congress ("playing a game of nug-a-nug!") laid the groundwork for a lifetime of suffering, for both partners.

John Harvey Kellogg, one of the most famous physicians of the late nineteenth century (and, as we will later learn, an absolute monster), was surprisingly sympathetic to the bride. Should this night be ugly, he warns the grooms, so shall be the rest of your married life.

"Many a woman dates the beginning of a life of suffering from the first night after marriage; and the mental suffering from the disgusting and even horrible recollections of that night, the events of which were scarred upon her mind as well as upon her body, have made her equally as wretched mentally as bodily. A learned French writer, in referring to this subject, says, 'The husband who begins with his wife by a rape is a lost man. He will never be loved.'"

Dr. Kellogg also shows uncommonly advanced thinking about a woman's right to her own body.

"The most heroic battle which many a man can fight is to protect his wife from his own lustful passions. Every young wife should know that it is her duty as well as her privilege to protect herself from the possible causes of life-long suffering. It is no woman's duty to surrender herself soul and body to her husband simply because he has promised to 'love and protect her.'"

Hudson agrees. Especially since, according to his experience, a lady's first time making love ("having your corn ground!") will be horrible no matter what you do.

"But you must be patient; never try to force matters at all; be as tender as a mother with her child; remember that the pleasures of married life will be anything but pleasures to the young maiden whom you have taken for your wife. Be as gentle as you may, they will cause her intense suffering; but if you are coarse, and brutal and rash, what torture they will be to her! They may even render your person ever after repulsive to her, so that she can never enjoy them with you. Such a feeling would deprive you of the enjoyment which you are expecting in the marriage relation, and might lead you to that ruinous step, infidelity to the marriage vow. Be wise, therefore; deny yourself at first, for the sake of future enjoyment; regard your wife's feelings and desires to the utmost."

Most experts were in agreement. Don't rape your wife, though technically it is your right; women are tetchy and hold grudges about that kind of thing.

PATENT FAMILY BEDSTEAD.

Some jokes don't age as well as others.

Dr. Virgil Primrose English went a step further and illustrated, in story form, just how such a night might unfold, particularly if the husband had well acquainted himself with prostitutes before his marriage. He, being a very stupid young man, assumes that the behavior of the paid sex worker is indicative of all women.

> "The harlots with whom he used to associate…flattered him regarding his sexual parts and powers, and the pleasure he gave them by intercourse, leading him to believe that he is as far superior to other men, as the sun is brighter than the moon. He realizes that his bride is virtuous, and inexperienced, and he congratulates himself upon the pleasure he is about to give her. His manner is more or less rough, and decidedly thoughtless as he attempts intercourse, and he is greatly surprised that the penis does not

Gertie was always up for anything.

readily enter the vagina, and when the bride displays evidence of pain, he thinks she is trying to deceive him, and he perseveres with redoubled persistence and vigor. This results in thoroughly frightening the bride, and in causing her intense suffering, and injuring her besides. She perhaps cries, and wishes she had never left her home, and he is disappointed and thoroughly disgusted, and thinks she is a little fool, and good for nothing. He doesn't see how she could be so unlike other women, and heartily wishes he had never seen her. The reader may imagine the rest."

I don't understand. The women I paid to say I was the best lover they ever had all said I was the best lover they ever had! And they've had a lot! So what's *your* deal, crybaby? If you'd stop sniveling and put your knees over your head like Dirty Gertie always does, you'd have a chance to enjoy this incredible experience I'm offering you!

As I said, a very stupid man, but yet not out of the realm of possibility.

Slaves and Graves

The dangers of a botched wedding night go beyond hurt feelings and sore soft bits. One way or another, bad sex kills. Says Dr. English,

> "The bride's beauty and vigor, the voluptuous figure and feelings, the hopes and plans, the love and sentiment, aye, even the interest in her husband, and the desire to live, will be quickly blasted....What husband can be happy, and hopeful, and light hearted, and picture a rosy future, when his wife is slowly sinking into her grave?"

And he's not just talking about the death of the soul. Similarly, Dr. Kellogg is a man prepared for the worst, including having your bride bleed out, right there in the honeymoon suite.

"The beginning as well as the full fruition of physiological marriage is accompanied by a more or less considerable amount of suffering on the part of the wife. This is in part due to the highly sensitive character of the mucous surfaces, and in part to the presence of the hymen. It should be borne in mind, however, that it is not only possible for such a rupture to take place, but that undue violence may give rise to a dangerous and even fatal hemorrhage, or to an equally dangerous inflammation."

A young John Harvey Kellogg, before he went completely starkers.

Perhaps this is what leads Dr. Kellogg to once again make the bold pronouncement that women are under no obligation to give a husband sex on demand. He decrees this slavery.

> "Many a woman is by her marriage vow introduced to a slavery far more galling and vastly more debasing than that which cost this nation years of civil war and hundreds of thousands of lives to abolish. The great majority of sufferers keep their troubles wholly secret, knowing that they have little sympathy to expect from those who believe this to be the proper lot of woman,—a burden imposed upon her by the curse; but now and then a woman's sufferings become too great to be longer borne in silence, and the facts come to the surface. It is high time that there was a change of public sentiment in reference to this matter. Of all the rights to which a woman is entitled, that of the custody of her own body is the most indubitable."

Oh, Dr. Kellogg. Why is it so often the absolute nutters who, between their blistering of six-year-old boys' penises so they won't masturbate and prescribing cornflakes to cure "hysteria," which isn't even really a thing, also speak sense so far ahead of their times? Granted, Dr. Kellogg would not have extended this support of a woman's right to her own body much further than the marriage bed. But it was very forward thinking for his era.

Mama, Don't Let Your Babies Grow Up Without Age-Appropriate Knowledge

What can be done to save a bride from the trauma of physical love ("bonestorming!")? Much, say the Victorian men whose minds dwell so completely on the state of women's private parts. (I might add here that I searched deeply for a book of this nature written for women by women. I am still convinced one must exist. I have not found it. So we are left once again to have the men teach us how to tend our peaks and valleys.)

Only a few of the authors, including Dr. Hoff, seem to have decoded the physical necessity of what is commonly known today as foreplay. Unless you caress and comfort your new wife, her sacred orifice will fold in upon its own tight and dusty walls.

"The condition of the female organs depends upon the condition of her mind, just as much as in the case of the male. He, however, is more sensual, and is more quickly roused. She is much less often or early ready. In its unexcited state, her vagina is lax, and its walls closed together and somewhat harsh and dry, little lubricating secretion being present. The modest bride has no de-

"All right, darling. I think my vestibule is prepared.
Thank you for your patience."

sire that this sacred vestibule to the great arcana of procreation shall be immediately invaded."

Yes, a husband's knowing that his wife must be cajoled and sweetly led to a state of submission that she may participate in an act the likes of which she's seen played out only in a barnyard ("grummeting!") is one good way to keep your marriage from imploding on its first night.

But the best defense should be instigated long before that night. A young husband may struggle to believe this, and most certainly not want to dwell on it in the heat of the moment, but his only real ally in this endeavor is the bride's mother. A mother's timely and prudent advice will maintain the purity of his bride's mind (no naughty pictures, no lascivious stories that will engorge her delicacy before he gets a chance to) while making sure she doesn't enter the marital chamber with the mentality of a frightened child. And to many "experts" of the time, a mother's common refusal to do this was a near-criminal act. Says Kellogg,

> "Many mothers seem to regard it a sort of virtue in their daughters that they are wholly ignorant of the import of marriage and its duties, and purposely keep them in ignorance, repressing in them any desire to acquire knowledge on the subject. Such a course we regard as criminally foolish, and the result of a perverted education on the part of the mothers of the present generation."

Even today, when every deodorant commercial and chewing-gum package is somehow saturated in sexuality, it is difficult for many mothers and daughters to discuss personal subjects. But asking a Victorian woman to violate a lifetime of shushed modesty to pollute her most innocent creation with the news that things are about to get real—well, it must have been excruciating. Who among us wants to be part of a dialog that begins:

"Remember, sweetheart, when we took Flossie to mate with the Gundersons' bull? And you thought he was killing her? And she was lowing away like she was in such pain? Well, aren't *you* in for a surprise!"

But Kellogg rightfully insists: it's practically a form of abuse to send a girl into the marital chamber without preparing her. What if she thinks he made "it" (the Featherbed Jig) up himself? The very fact that he could concoct such a perversion will crush her soul and send her screaming into the night!

"Don't be glum, dearest! I always like to think of it as a good time to go over the household budget in my head!"

"On this subject every woman should have full and reliable information before entering the marriage relation. Mothers should not think that because they were ignorant, their daughters should be equally so. Thousands of women might have saved themselves from life-long suffering had they received the proper instruction at the right time."

Dr. Hoff paints an even more heart-wrenching picture. A poor girl jumps into her marriage bed in her new bridal peignoir made of the heaviest-quality cambric, with eleven separate rows of tucks, ribbons,

And sometimes being forewarned just makes for depressing wedding photography.

flounces, beading, Hamburg embroidery, and point de Paris lace, all set to snuggle the daylights out of her handsome groom. (Because heaven knows those bridal trousseaus don't allow for much other movement.) And inside the bed what does she find? Mortification, that's what.

"What wonder that some brides have come to their mothers and female friends after marriage, to whom they had a right to look for advice and warning concerning these things, and, with passionate tears of shame and indignation, have reproached them bitterly, saying: 'Oh, why did you not tell me! Why should an innocent girl be thus deceived and outraged with allurements of false happiness!'"

Allurements of false happiness! She had been led to believe that there were no penises, and now that beautiful dream is dashed to bits. For shame, mothers. The girl is going to discover that pernicious member one way or another. How cruel of you to send her into the wilds of marriage and not even suggest that, like the concealed but deadly poison dart frog of South America, there are penises a-lurk in this apparent paradise, and they are ready to strike!

Pleasure Is a Pulsating Womb

So aside from foreknowledge, and fore*play,* what other measures can be taken to ensure a pleasant wedding-night experience?

This is important. Don't let him try to crunch you up into any weird, unnatural positions. James Ashton doesn't want to see that peculiar tube of yours curving in the wrong directions. After all, creative positioning during the venereal act ("frickle-frackle!") can cause fungal growth, cancer, and death.

> "Any unnatural performance of this act is apt to impair the health of the female, and many women have been seriously in-
jured and rendered miserable for life by the beastliness of their husbands in this respect. Unnatural positions will cause derangements and bearing down of the womb…and sometimes will originate tumors and fungi in the private parts. A woman of delicate mould and constitution might be fatally injured in this manner; and no female, however robust, can enjoy sexual intercourse except in the position intended by Nature."

To be clear, Ashton explains the one *true* position, ordained by God and Nature, for amorous congress ("jiggery-pokery!").

> "The natural position to which we have alluded suggests itself to every married pair who possess the most remote particle of love

for each other. But to make it unmistakable, we would say, that the female should lie upon her back, with her legs straight down or if the legs are raised, they should be but slightly elevated. All other positions are unnatural and unhealthy. I could illustrate this fact by several cases in point, but the details are too disgusting."

Having the woman's legs firmly locked downward seems as if it would make an already tricky act nearly impossible, but you, my virgin flower, are not to know that. Luckily other experts, like Dr. Hoff, allow the female to slightly draw her knees up. That extra bit of berth may be quite helpful.

But don't go any further with your acrobatics, now. Just so that you can be certain to never, say in a moment of passion, accidentally perform any of the forbidden marital connections ("a rough mow!"), Dr. Ashton hints at them.

"Suffice it then to say, that I have known females suffering from painful diseases caused by sexual connection in a standing position, in a position where their partners approached them from behind, and also in one case where the woman was forced or persuaded to lie on her back with her knees up against her chest. No female can desire such intercourse as this, because she cannot enjoy it."

Hush! Upon your lips is the question "How in the world would you presume to know *that*, sir?" *and there it will stay!* He knows because he has probably seen many an unhappy woman with female trouble, asked them what their sexual positions of late have been, and thereby drawn the obvious conclusion. That's called science. At least in this century. To these men.

Besides, everyone knows that there is only one way a woman can fully enjoy connubial thrusts. A woman who does not reach a state of polite ecstasy during intercourse is not having her parts properly manipulated.

If you think this indicates a lack of clitoral stimulation, that is your second mistake. Your first is thinking about a clitoris at all, you tawdry thing. No, it is commonly known that clitoral stimulation is no more than an exterior irritation women must do their best to ignore. Rather, the seat of female climax is, most naturally, the seat of life itself: her womb.

Says Ashton:

"Many women say that they experience very little sexual feeling, and that the act of copulation is to them a matter of indifference. This is because the mouth of the Womb is not reached or touched by the glans of the male organ; and the pleasurable sensation of the female is then confined to a slight irritation of the Clitoris and Nymphaea [labia], in the private parts.

"When the amorous sensations of the female are excited during connection, the womb becomes engorged with blood, and moves up and down in the Vagina, bringing the neck in contact with the glans of the

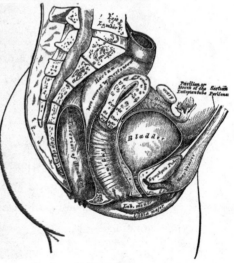

Quick guide: peculiar tube leads to sloshy baby hole. Ignore the rest; it's just there to confuse you.

male organ, and this contact, if not too violent, is the perfection of sexual indulgence for both parties."

The problem is you've not got your womb bouncing good and proper. If you were performing the act as it was intended, your uterus would begin to bounce and slosh like a buoy on a lake full of motorboats, likely in anticipation of the small human who may soon lodge within it. That is the only way a woman can experience true sexual fulfillment.

Warning: Do Not Have Relations ("Rumbusticating!")

After a large meal, "instances having been known of apoplexy [cerebral hemorrhage or stroke] being induced by the excitement of connection, being superadded to the stimulative influence of wine and food."   *— Hoff*

While either partner is drunk, because "idiocy and numerous nervous maladies are liable to appear in the offspring of an intoxicated father or mother."   *— Jefferis & Nichols*

After great physical or mental exercise, as "several cases are recorded where apoplexy occurred from over-excitement during the sexual act, and there have been instances where blindness, insanity, and even death, ensued from too excessive agitation."   *— Hoff*

Often: "The best writers lay down the rule for the government of the marriage-bed, that sexual indulgence should only occur about once in a week or ten days, and this of course applies only

Leonardo da Vinci, one magnificent bastard

to those who enjoy a fair degree of health. But it is a hygienic and physiological fact that those who indulge only once a month receive a far greater degree of the intensity of enjoyment than those who indulge their passions more frequently. Much pleasure is lost by excesses where much might be gained by temperance, giving rest to the organs for the accumulation of nervous force."

— *Jefferis & Nichols*

When thinking of more important things: "When a man is performing this act, if his thoughts wander, the product will be feeble, and if his wife become pregnant the off-spring will be inferior....In further confirmation of this theory, history informs us that some of the greatest men the world ever saw were bastards; children begotten with vigor, and when the minds of the parents are supposed to have been absorbed in the one idea of a loving sexual embrace."

—Ashton

His Homespun Harlot

I will devote nearly every word of this epistle to cautioning you against immodesty. You have learned to dress yourself in enough obfuscating layers of steel and wool to make Kevlar look like a mesh belly shirt. You have learned how to hold your head so as to avoid sexually exciting strangers. You have learned the shame of your body and its functions. Men were mostly the ones who taught you this. And now, with the setting of the sun, you're to forget every word of it.

"Many men...find their energies palsied by the frigid conduct of their brides. Many women, moving in a respectable sphere of life, have the idea that it is unbecoming and indecorous to meet the embraces of their husbands, or to shew any solicitude in the matter; thus directly opposing the dictates of nature, and setting themselves in opposition to one of the main purposes for which they were created. There was much pertinence in the saying attributed to the daughter-in-law of Pythagoras, 'that the woman who goes to bed with a man, must put off her modesty with her petticoat, and put it on again with the same.'"

—Culverwell

Kick all the feminine modesty urged upon you by men to the curb. Because now those same men need you to get frisky. Or else they will spend the grocery money purchasing a household full of shame and disease in some noxious red-light fleshpot. And it will be your fault. After all, writes Hoff, "many a man who was honestly inclined to keep inviolate his marriage vows, has been driven by his wife's cold repulses to gratify his desire in the embraces of prostitutes."

You heard the man. Now that you know what to expect, the best thing you can do is find a way to make your peace with the inevitable as soon as possible. If you won't do it, well, there are plenty of Dirty Gerties and Fannie Funbags willing to spread good times and gonorrhea to your neglected husband.

Fair? Is it fair, *cherie?* Oh, my sweet girl, what book have *you* been reading?

But wait, one last word, from Dr. Culverwell, he who decries a woman who behaves in her bed as she does everywhere else in her life.

"Slow? While I'll beat you yet!" That's the scrumpy spirit, old girl!

He also has no tolerance for the man who doesn't give his bride a satisfying marital consummation ("scrumping!"):

> "No man has a right to defraud, by the assumption of manhood, a female of her expected portion, the fair and honorable consummation of the nuptial ceremony; and if he do, from choice or infirmity, the sin and consequences be on his own head."

A lady has needs, too. Thank you, Dr. Culverwell.

One of those needs, of course, is not to die in childbirth, which happened horribly often in the early days of the nineteenth century. So how do you go about satisfying your marital duties without risking your life, or turning your uterus into a candy machine that dispenses baby-shaped gum balls? Let's learn, shall we?

9

Birth Control
and Other Affronts to God

· AND THE VILLAIN STIEL PURSUES HER ·

*Y*ou're probably already pregnant. There isn't a whole lot else to do for entertainment in the evenings. In no time at all, you can expect to be expecting. You're going to get "k'napped," to use a term of the day. The infantry is coming. You'll be set to launch. Plead the belly. Lay a chit. You've been playing tricks and gone lumpy!

Sometimes Natural Isn't Best

If the prospect vexes you, good; you've been paying attention. Giving birth in a time when the greatest and only obstetrical innovation available is the newly fashioned baby-yanking forceps is not going to meet your twenty-first-century standards for a satisfactory birth plan.

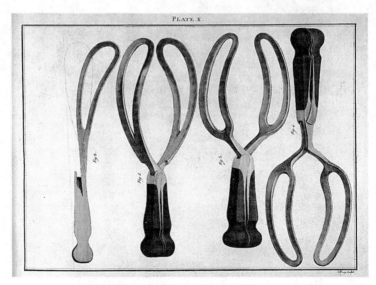

Late-eighteenth-century forceps

Although, for the record, you should be very grateful for these forceps. They really were better than nothing. In fact, *not* using them changed the course of British history. At the beginning of the nineteenth century they were not popular. They existed, but it was the fashion among doctors to take a "conservative management" approach to child-birth, what the twenty-first century would proudly refer to as natural childbirth. So forceps were not used when King George IV's only legit-imate daughter and heir, Princess Charlotte, went into a fifty-hour labor in 1817. The baby was sideways, and the doctors made no attempt to turn him. The child was stillborn, Charlotte died of internal hemorrhaging, and the overseeing physician soon committed suicide. In the wake of this tragedy, noninterference lost its popularity. And subsequently, with no heir, King George's crown passed through a younger brother down to the only remaining royal descendant, a young woman named Victoria.

It could very well be that the whole reason there is a Victorian era is that those forceps weren't used. Victoria herself had no prob-lem engaging whatever interventions were available, including being knocked out by chloroform (thereby making pain management during childbirth socially acceptable), and delivered nine babies with no fatal-ities. Most women weren't so lucky, especially in a culture that did not encourage robustness in fine ladies.

Why Bother with Babies?

Now, if you'd ended up farther west, you might not mind being afflict-ed with numerous pregnancies so much. You might even be fine with birthing yourself a whole *plague* of babies. If you were a nineteenth-century farmer's wife, yanking your existence from the stubborn mud of a Nebraskan winter with chapped and bleeding hands, you'd proba-bly barely notice if someone tossed another baby atop that mess.

If only the three-year-old didn't have such spindly little arms.
She can barely hold a single bushel of tobacco leaves.

Having many children was an investment for the rural and moderately poor. You were financing your own retirement with every ounce of mother's milk your toothless little millstones sucked down. By the time your oldest daughter was seven, she'd be doing a quarter of your housework. By the time all of the children were out of diapers, your main job would be cooking and barking orders, ideally. And when you were too old to work, it would then be *their* turn to shove milk into *your* toothless mouth.

But that is not where you landed. In the Victorian life you've been given, your retirement was settled generations ago, with annuities rolling into your husband's bank account in perpetuity. Your survival is not so dependent on physical labor that you must breed your own workforce. So what need have you for children?

Well, because you want them, of course. They're life's greatest joy! They're your legacy! Women who complain about the trials of moth-

Living treasures. Now take them back to their containment area.
These drapes are new, and the children are getting the porridge
stink of youth all over them.

erhood simply do not have the fortitude you have. "Fortitude" is your
collective name for the nurse, nannies, and governess in your employ.
If you wish, you need view your children, spit-shined and polished,
only one hour a day, after which Nurse will thrash them soundly if they
are not on their finest behavior. Children are treasures!

But for heaven's sake, you only need two or three. It's indecent to
have many more, no offense to Her Majesty's brood (she averaged about
one birth for every two years her husband lived). But she was providing
English heads to fit under the many crowns of Europe. Granted, her
grandchildren would end up raining death from above on each other's
countries shortly after her passing, in World War I. Family reunions

Ugh. Ribbit.

must have been terribly awkward. But Her Majesty *had* to do it, for the sake of the empire. It didn't work, but we love her for her sacrifice. Especially since Queen Victoria detested pregnancy and thought babies were gross. To her grown daughter she wrote:

> "I like them better than I did, if they are nice and pretty....Abstractedly, I have no tender *[sic]* for them till they have become a little human; an ugly baby is a very nasty object—and the prettiest is frightful when undressed. Until about 4 months; in short as long as they have their big body and little limbs and that terrible froglike action."

But for you, since you have no empire to populate or farm to run, having gobs of babies is just declaring your poor self-control to the neighborhood. It's like putting out your booze bottles for recycling so everyone can see how much you drink, except it's sex.

The best thing that could be said for childbirth in the 1800s was that it wasn't as deadly as it used to be. There was practically, oh—say, a 70 percent chance you and the child would live? Nineteenth-century childbirth is a game of Russian roulette where even if you win, your perineum will be badly torn with no antibiotic ointment to heal it and where for the rest of your life you'll tinkle when you sneeze.

So I certainly can't argue if you've decided you want no more children. Medical science, however, is amused at your decision and wishes you the best of luck with that. It is still a very long time before Gregory

Pincus and John Rock will completely change the world by inventing a dependable birth-control pill, which becomes available in 1960. So your options are less scientific and more…creative.

They are also considered by some Victorians—or at least the loudest Victorians—to be unethical, un-Christian, and sometimes fatally unhealthy.

Sterility, Colicky Uteri, and Weazened Monsters

The most obvious way to avoid producing an embarrassing amount of sexual by-products (children) was to avoid overindulgence in sex. After all, having intercourse for carnal reasons alone is like allowing your husband to use you as a prostitute. Which is pretty much the only way

Graphic, yes, dear, but you can take it. At least you'd better be able to.

to keep him away from real prostitutes. Thus, most people who opposed birth control attempted to inspire medical fears instead of ethical ones.

Especially hated was the most common method, withdrawal. Men of science claimed this abomination was no different than practicing one of the most deadly habits known to mankind. No, not smoking, don't be ridiculous. Smoking improves asthma and makes you look distinguished. No, the *other* most deadly habit. Jefferis and Nichols, speaking once again from *Search Lights on Health,* explain:

> "Probably no one means is more serious in its results than the practice of withdrawal, or the discharge of the semen externally to the vagina. The act is incomplete and unnatural, and is followed by results similar to and as disastrous as those consequent upon masturbation. In the male it may result in impotence, in the female in sterility. In both sexes many nervous symptoms are produced, such as headache, defective vision, dyspepsia, insomnia, loss of memory, etc. Very many cases of uterine diseases can be attributed solely to this practice."

We are grateful to Jefferis and Nichols for recognizing that our ignorance of medical matters, and apparently the female body, would make it impossible for us to understand how withdrawal produces such a rainbow of ailments and therefore burdening us with no further details about the connection. However, other doctors point to the fact that a woman cannot orgasm if withdrawal is practiced, and it is this lack of orgasm that causes nearly all female maladies.

If it seems to you, at first blush, that these men don't know how female orgasms work, I would beg you to hold your tongue. These men, unlike you, are secure in the knowledge that the clitoris, far from being the seat of true womanly pleasure, isn't much more than a puny vestigial penis that probably shouldn't even be there. Have you ever considered that *you're* the one orgasming incorrectly?

Orson Squire Fowler, who we are most privileged to consult, for he is a fount of candidness in a cagey world, can illuminate this in even more detail.

> "Woman suffers most from this vice [withdrawal] because her organs are adapted to act for a longer period. It provokes in her all diseases of her genital organs, from simple inflammation to the most serious derangements—metritis, tumors, polypi, uterine colics, neurosis, cancers, mammal and ovarian diseases, sterility, leucorrhoea, etc. When I review all the diseases of the women I have attended, I believe three-fourths of them were caused by the practice of frauds in sexual intercourse, and that, in most cases, they can with certainty be attributed to it."

A full three-fourths of the diseases in the women he has attended are the result of engaging in nonreproductive sex! That's— that is an impressive number of gynecological exams and diagnoses for a phrenologist! Almost a disturbing number. I had assumed he concentrated his attention on head bumps, not lady bumps. It appears there was some crossover.

The tragic final stages of semen deprivation

And not only women suffered, explains John Kellogg. He believes withdrawal is where "monsters" (once the actual clinical term for children with birth defects) come from. (Note: Dr. Kellogg quotes many other authors in his work, but he is a bit lackadaisical about keeping them cited. According to Kellogg, the following quote comes from a man identified as "distinguished Mayer.")

"So, who knows if the infants, too often feeble and weazen, are not the fruit of these in themselves incomplete procreations, and disturbed by preoccupations foreign to the generic act? Is it not reasonable to suppose that the creative power, not meeting in its

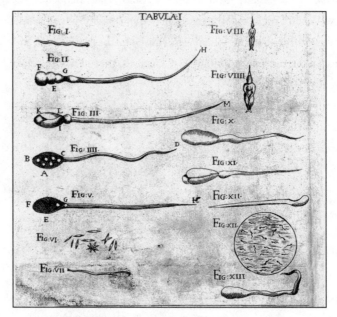

Sad and bitter sperm, which, by the way,
actually have the tiny miserable humans they're going to grow into
already living inside them.

disturbed functions the conditions necessary for the elaboration
of a normal product, the conception might be from its origin imperfect, and the being which proceeded therefrom, one of those
monsters which are described in treatises on teratology?"

I am not a doctor, and I will admit I struggle to follow the word-
ing of this excerpt, but I believe the theory runs something like this:
should a lady be accidentally splashed with the sullen, sickly sperm
that slops forth from the male body during the practice of withdrawal,
that sperm, having been sourced from a place of most bitter melancholy, will halfheartedly lug itself toward the female egg, stumble into
a peevish germination, and produce an unhealthy zygote.

Well, I certainly can't prove that's *not* the case.

Kellogg also quotes a Dr. Francis Devay, to better describe the pitiful state of the female "apparatus" if it is not granted an ejaculation.

"A profound stimulation is felt through the entire apparatus; the
uterus, fallopian tubes, and ovaries enter into a state of orgasm, a
storm which is not appeased by the natural crisis; a nervous su-
perexcitation persists. There occurs, then, what would take place
if, presenting food to a famished man, one should snatch it from
his mouth after having thus violently excited his appetite. The
sensibilities of the womb and the entire reproductive system are
teased for no purpose. It is to this cause, too often repeated, that
we should attribute the multiple neuroses, those strange affections
which originate in the genital system of woman."

Snatching food from a starving man's mouth? Fallopian tubes in an
orgasmic storm? And shouldn't the clitoris be at least a token piece of
this famished apparatus? These questions you may be asking yourself,

I know. You might even be thinking that the men of this era are greatly, *greatly,* overestimating the awesome power of their semen by believing its mere presence will bring you to a state of coital nirvana. But shush, dear. Without possessing the potent life nectar yourself, you are really in no position to judge its qualities.

Prepare to Meet Your God: Onanism and Property Extant

As I said before, it was difficult to convince people that preventing conception was unethical. But that didn't stop a determined ragtag group of righteous men from trying to show that there *was* inherent sin in contraception. Kellogg takes us through the earliest known record of this evil practice.

Representing the debilitated state of the body from the effects of Onanism or Self-pollution.

The result of onanism

"Conjugal Onanism.—The soiling of the conjugal bed by the shameful maneuvers to which we have made allusion, is mentioned for the first time in Gen. 38 : 6, and following verses: 'And it came to pass, when he [Onan] went in unto his brother's wife, that he spilled it on the ground, lest that he should give seed to his brother. And the thing which he did displeased the Lord; wherefore he slew him.'"

In the Bible story Kellogg refers to, a man named Er was killed by God for his wickedness, details nondisclosed. Onan was his brother, and it was his duty to take his brother's place and impregnate his sister-in-law, Tamar. Biblical scholars say that if Tamar had conceived, her child would be considered Er's and would inherit handsomely. If she did not, Onan, the next in line, would inherit instead. Onan purposefully withheld his fecundity, spilling it on the ground instead. So God killed him too. (Incidentally, should you purchase yourself a little pet bird, as was popular practice at this time, Onan would be a cracking name for the little beggar, as caged birds are constantly spilling their seeds on the ground.)

The inference being, God prefers that you not practice withdrawal. Orson Squire Fowler would prefer this also. I leave it to you to decide whose wrath is more frightful.

"PREVENTING CONCEPTION OUTRAGES EVERY SEXUAL LAW. Think you, after God has created you men and women, and ordained all this creative machinery solely to secure reproduction, you can thwart and cheat Him without incurring His retribution commensurate with His highest law you break? Prepare to meet your God, ye who persist. Every argument for it is futile....Right bearing never exhausts but always improves mothers, and large families are the best pieces of **property** extant."

Besides, everyone knows it is the childless women who live lives of pointlessness riddled with disease and brain fever! Having many children is the healthiest thing a woman can do!

According to Jefferis and Nichols,

"Having children under proper circumstances never ruins the health and happiness of any woman. In fact, womanhood is incomplete without them. She may have a dozen or more, and still have better health than before marriage."

Well, sometimes there is a general wearing down of the reproductive

Mother of twelve after removing corset

organs if a woman produces a dozen or more children. Among other maladies, the prolapsed uterus was very common in this era. The best way I can describe it to you is to have you imagine your reproductive tract as a tube sock. Now turn it inside out, and let it dangle there. Prolapse.

Thwarting Sperm

Of course these men were not fools. They understood there were cases where it was not advisable to have more children. There was one method that even the most stalwart internal-ejaculation supporter could endorse, and that was temperance. If you want no more children, have no more sexual intercourse. We are, after all, men, not animals.

Well, technically men, humans, are animals. Actually more than technically. As I mentioned, the abstinence option was not popular or successful. Even when paired with the healthful suggestion that couples sleep in separate beds to avoid temptation (a very expensive option, beyond most families' financial means).

Medical men like Jefferis and Nichols who did not want to anger God or the United States government (publishing information about birth control was illegal for much of the nineteenth century, as we shall see) often offered timetables of when a woman was most fertile, least fertile, and even temporarily "sterile."

"Another Provision of Nature.—For a certain period between her monthly illness, every woman is sterile. Conception may be

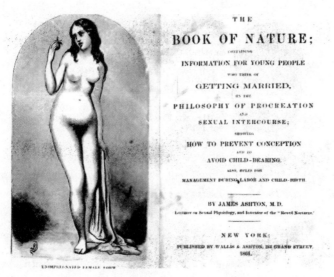

THE

BOOK OF NATURE;

CONTAINING

INFORMATION FOR YOUNG PEOPLE

WHO THINK OF

GETTING MARRIED,

ON THE

PHILOSOPHY OF PROCREATION

AND

SEXUAL INTERCOURSE;

SHOWING

HOW TO PREVENT CONCEPTION

AND TO

AVOID CHILD-BEARING.

ALSO, RULES FOR

MANAGEMENT DURING LABOR AND CHILD-BIRTH.

BY JAMES ASHTON, M.D.

Lecturer on Sexual Physiology, and Inventor of the "Reveil Nocturne."

NEW YORK:

PUBLISHED BY WALLIS & ASHTON, 313 GRAND STREET.
1861.

UNIMPREGNATED FEMALE FORM

avoided by refraining from coition except for this particular number of days, and there will be no evasion of normal Intercourse, no
resort to disgusting practices, and nothing degrading."

This generous provision of Nature often proved not generous
enough, which is why even today, reference to the rhythm method is
usually followed with a baby-laden punch line.

Women have been trying to block sperm from egg since the moment they suspected what the meeting of the two resulted in. The
methods and ingredients have varied over the centuries and around
the globe, but the basics have been the same. Sperm: put up a barrier,
wash it out, or try to kill it before it reaches its prize. Dr. James Ashton,
in his remarkably informative and detailed *The Book of Nature,* found
no sin nor ethical dilemma in a married couple trying to limit family
size. Here are a few methods he recommends, along with one suggestion from fellow doctor H. P. Monroe:

No. 8R702 Ladies' Silk Sponges,
very fine, regular form. Each....**20c**
No. 8R705 Selected, with silk
netting cover and silk cord. Each.**25c**
No. 8R708 Extra fine, small medium; ladies' cup shaped silk sponges.
Each..........................**35c**
No. 8R711 Superfine, large ladies'
cup shaped sponges, specially selected forms and shapes. Each..**50c**
Bleach Mediterranean Sponges,
for toilet and bath.

Now, this Sears, Roebuck catalog has no idea what you're going to want to do with a cup-shaped ladies' sponge with netting and string; it simply sells them. I think it's assumed they're used in craft projects.

Sponge and Spermicide

"Procure a fine sponge at a drug-store, and cut off a piece of it about the size of a walnut; then make a fine silk string by twisting together some threads of sewing silk; tie one end of the string to the piece of sponge; wet the sponge in a weak solution of sulphate of iron, or of any of the solutions before mentioned as fatal to the animalculae of the Semen. Before connection, insert the piece of sponge far up into your person. You can place it entirely out of the way by the use of a smooth stick of the proper size and shape. The string will hang out, but will be no obstacle. After the act is over, you withdraw the sponge."

Douching

"The judicious use of an ordinary female syringe, with cold water alone, or a weak solution of white vitriol or other stringent in cold water, immediately after coition, will in most cases prevent concep-tion. By the use of this article a female may inject as much fluid as she pleases, through an elastic tube, quite as far up into her person as is necessary. The mixture should be prepared beforehand, and, with the syringe, kept by her bed-side, as success often depends upon promptness in using it."

Homemade Spermicide Recipes

The recipes in Ashton's book contained fairly innocuous ingredients: alum, zinc, iron, rainwater. They also...probably didn't work great. Especially in the case of douching. Besides the greased-lightning movement of sperm, the aroused tissue of the vaginal wall stretches out, then wrinkles and folds back up again when arousal has passed, leaving infinite crannies for sperm to sequester itself in, where even a very thorough flushing cannot reach. This is probably one of the reasons quickness is advised. Sometimes, as in the recipe below, medical men suggest putting the sperm killer in place before it is needed.

Dr. H. P. Monroe shares his remedy in an 1897 volume of the periodical *The Medical World:*

RUBBER GOODS.
Syringes, Etc.

The S., R. & Co.'s Gem Fountain Syringe, made from good quality rubber, with hard rubber fittings, four hard rubber pipes, including large irrigating pipe, in a neat box, long rubber tubing with patent shut off.
No. 8R753   2 quarts, each..50c
No. 8R756   3 quarts, each..63c
No. 8R759   4 quarts, each..68c
Shipping weight, 18 ounces.

One of many syringes (douche bags with nozzles) available for general health purposes. Nothing else. Sears, Roebuck supports clean, healthy rectums and vaginal canals. Nothing else.

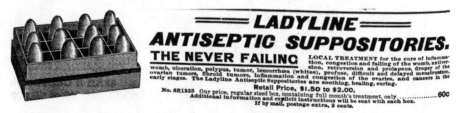

══LADYLINE══
ANTISEPTIC SUPPOSITORIES.
THE NEVER FAILING LOCAL TREATMENT for the cure of inflammation, congestion and falling of the womb, antiversion, retroversion and prolapsus, dropsy of the ovarian tumors, fibroid tumors, inflammation and congestion of the ovaries, and cancers in the early stages. The Ladyline Antiseptic Suppositories are soothing, healing, curing.
Retail Price, $1.50 to $2.00.
No. 8R1255 Our price, regular sized box, containing full month's treatment, only.............60c
Additional information and explicit instructions will be sent with each box.
If by mail, postage extra, 3 cents.

Antiseptic vaginal suppositories. Just for cleanliness. They kill—germs. And possibly things that rhyme with "germ."

"I make a vaginal suppository of cocoa butter, into which I incorporate from 6 to 10 per cent, of boracic acid and the same amount of tannic acid. These suppositories should weigh from y₂ dram to one dram each. From three to five minutes before congress one of these suppositories is introduced into the vagina, and pushed well up against the cervix. The cocoa butter having melted and set the boracic and tannic acids free, they act as an effectual germicide, thus destroying the spermatozoa."

Scrotum Bondage (Don't...Don't Do This One)

"Some men tie up the scrotum to prevent a discharge of Semen, and thus hope to avoid impregnating the female; but this method is exceedingly hurtful, as it forces the discharge into the bladder, from whence it passes off with the urine. Such a practice will in a short time so derange the procreative organs as to send all the Semen into the bladder as fast as it generates, and the effect on health will be a wasting away of vitality in the same manner as if the patient constantly practiced self-pollution."

I don't know how much of this information from Ashton beyond the words "exceedingly hurtful" is accurate, but really, that first part is probably all that need be said.

Withdrawal

But the most effective prevention *The Book of Nature* recommends is, of course, the one with the greatest history of causing God to slay its practitioners. Ashton does not believe withdrawal should be equated with onanism. "This plan injures neither party," he writes, "nor does it really diminish the pleasurable sensations of connection." And "if properly performed, the act of coition is as pleasurable, as healthy and as complete as it can be when the Semen is fully injected." He is even prepared to address questions of cleanliness so as not to disgust ladies of refinement. (Again, there seems to be some misunderstanding that once a woman is given the gift of semen, even internally, it vaporizes into pure light and she does not need to deal with it again. We know this not to be the case, darling, but let us not disabuse these gentlemen of their pleasant illusion.)

"The cleanliness of this practice is also a great desideratum, as females of any degree of refinement can understand. I would then suggest to married people the following rule: Always carry to bed a clean napkin, which is to be kept in the hand of the male during the nuptial act. It will then be a very easy matter to place this napkin in a proper position to receive the Semen on with-drawal, at the instant it would otherwise be injected into the body of the female. If you do it at the proper moment, no pleasure is lost to either party; and habit will soon make you expert in this respect."

If only it were as easy as that, good sir. But you have neglected to sat-isfactorily account for the presence of monster sperm and spasmodic vagina disease caused by lack of semen supplements, or to give us the confidence that we will not be slain, as precedent suggests we might.

Objects of No-sire

Other medical texts list devices to use against pregnancy: the condom, of course, which was just making its transformation from animal-skin sheath to horrid thick rubber male-member mackinaw. It was unpopular, for it slipped, broke, diminished sensation, and gave the female no control over the situation.

One doctor, F. F. Jackson, writing to *The Medical World* (volume 15, 1897), lists other devices he has encountered in his practice, and his reasons for dismissing them.

"The use of the hood, or 'French Pessaire' [cervical cap], for the female, requires too much skill in its adjustment, so that many times it fails to accomplish its purpose.

The aluminum button, to be placed in the uterus, is of more recent origin. The objection to this is it can only be used when the uterus is perfectly free from all discharge [this likely refers to an early form of the IUD]."

Wishbone-style pessary. Used both for thumbtacking prolapses back into place and (potentially) birth control.

There was another reason for not using these objects in attempts to thwart conception: simply put, because they were in fact objects, ones that needed to be procured, sent for, *mailed.* Clear into the twentieth century, it was illegal to mail contraceptives, or information about contraceptives, in America. How *The Medical World,* though not intended for the public, even managed *its* distribution is a mystery to me.

This information wasn't always illegal. *The Book of Nature,* which has given us such detailed information, was published and distributed legally in 1861. Twelve years later, that would have been impossible. Why? Because of one man. Hailed by some as the last great Puritan Christian of America, considered by most others an arrogant, draconian, pharisaical busybody who believed he had a right to nestle himself between the bedsheets of every couple in the country. Anthony Comstock.

What Comstockery Is This?

"Comstockery" is defined as "excessive opposition to supposed immorality in the arts; prudery." It's something a gruff old English teacher might bark out at a school-board meeting where it is decided to ban all books that contain the word "climax." Including *Dumbo*. Utter Comstockery.

Anthony Comstock's mother died when he was only ten years old. She had been a fiercely religious woman, and after her death her son vowed to make her spirit proud. Comstock prayed for guidance, God's love, and, above all, purity.

When Comstock's brother was killed at Gettysburg, Comstock enlisted in his place. He was nowhere near the front line, but rather in Florida, living in barracks with other young soldiers. Comstock dis-

"What is that perverted trash you're reading? Moby-DICK? Ho, ho...not on my watch, mister."

covered this environment to be much more sweaty and sweary than the one he'd been reared in. The men had very little interest in purity, though Comstock and the Young Men's Christian Association tried to urge it upon them.

BAILEY'S
FINE CANDIES,
45 WEST STREET, BOSTON. 204

Saints preserve us. Flashy graphics, promises of sweets, and a child sliding out of a round orifice. Absolute filth.

After the war he went to New York City as a clerk. There he found a city absolutely writhing in sin. (Comstock, it should be noted, was not just against birth control and sexual sins. In his published works he warned against the inherent sin found in novels, patent medicine, state lotteries, poker, pool, children's storybooks, newspapers that reported crime too engagingly, the theater, flashy advertisements, candy stores, and "Liberals.")

The story goes that a good friend of his bought a dirty book, which inflamed his lust, which took him to a brothel, which gave him syphilis, which killed him in a most humiliating, flesh-rotting manner. Apparently, one of Comstock's first takedowns was to find the bookseller who sold his friend the book and have him arrested.

Comstock began seeking out vice in all forms, sniffing out brothels and gambling halls and purveyors of contraception, calling the police on every squalid hole of moral turpitude he found. And when that wasn't enough, he headed off to Washington, D.C., with intentions to amend an existing bill that made it illegal to send obscene material through the mail. He believed the existing definition of "obscene" was not nearly inclusive enough.

Was Anthony Comstock a policeman? A lawyer? A preacher, even? No, no. Just a man who believed that lust was the root of all sins and that people would *not* sin if there were no opportunities to do so. It turned out, that's all it took to change the law of our country. When all was said and done, the new act—passed in 1873 and popularly known as the Comstock Law—read thusly:

"Every obscene, lewd, or lascivious book, pamphlet, picture, paper, writing, print, or other publication of an indecent character, and every article or thing designed or intended for the prevention of conception or procuring of abortion, and every article or thing intended or adapted for any indecent or immoral use, and every written or printed card, circular, book, pamphlet, advertisement, or notice of any kind giving information, directly or indirectly, where, or how, or of whom, or by what means, any of the hereinbefore mentioned matters, articles, or things may be obtained or made…are hereby declared to be non-mailable matter, and shall not be conveyed in the mails, nor delivered from any post-office, nor by any letter-carrier."

He was not able to ban candy stores.

However, now you couldn't advertise products or services related to human sexuality or contraception, and you certainly couldn't send condoms, pessaries (except possibly to doctors who could prove they were giving them to patients to help them pin their prolapsed organs back into place), or spermicides through the mail.

Technically the new law didn't make the practice of contraception illegal. Just as technically Prohibition didn't make it illegal to *drink* booze, only to make, sell, or transport it. If you could still somehow get your hands on it, enjoy.

The overall effect of this law was to put contraception in the same

Advertisements like this British example,
which subtly promoted everything from abortion potions to condoms,
were precisely the publications that Comstock wanted to
keep out of the hands of the public with his bill.

psychological category as the most wretched filth printable and deadly, illegal abortions.

And no, Comstock did not consider birth control an alternative to abortions (to many Christians of the time, preventing a life was the same as murdering one).

He did not associate birth control with half-dead mothers of twelve hungry babes whose drunk husbands kept impregnating them with yet another feeble life that would starve and wither.

To him, contraception made it possible for people to have *sex without consequence.* And by people, he mostly meant whores and the once-innocent young men they defiled, who in turn went out and defiled the whole world.

Much of Comstock's writings defending his crusade are devoted to listing the crimes and vices committed by youth who he believed were inflamed to sin by obscene literature and dens of iniquity. This is the only reason he can think of for why young people turn to crime. You, with 150 years of social-scientific knowledge that Comstock did not have, may think to ask a question he did not: "What sort of homes did these youths come from?"

In the early twentieth century, Margaret Sanger asked and answered that question. Her answer came from years spent helping the poorest of the poor. The young offenders Comstock pointed to as victims of unmonitored lust most often came from crushing poverty, from homes where there were too many mouths to feed and parents too exhausted to care for the children they could not prevent themselves from having.

Sanger was indicted in 1914 for publishing birth-control pamphlets. Comstock died in 1915 with his law still on the books, and Sanger defeated in court. That balance did not hold long. A year after his death Sanger opened a clinic, part of a greater association she founded that became Planned Parenthood. Comstock might have won the birth-control battle. But he did not win the war.

When Women Make Decisions: Humanity's Greatest Threat

Comstock and his supporters aside, Victorian people were not all that opposed to birth control. In fact, by the standards of some, such as Mr. Fowler (who had three children by three wives), they were entirely too much in favor of it, especially the women. Fowler laments the folly of those who desire small families.

> "Most married pairs are stark mad against issue. Whoever can patent a means of enjoying fully without conceiving or injuring, could soon become the richest man in Christendom, so highly would men prize and pay for it, and women the most, purity and conscience to the contrary, and most married are insanely bent on small families."

It is perhaps because of this—how truly desperately people wanted to limit their families—that many learned men in the medical community claimed that even if they *knew* a good way to prevent conception, they ought never, ever tell anyone seeking it. Especially women.

After one doctor writes *The Medical World* with his proprietary spermicide recipe, he ends his letter with this warning:

> "But let me caution you never to write a prescription for this remedy. The knowledge of these remedies should not become public property, for few women would ever consent to endure the

pangs of child birth if they were in possession of the knowledge of so simple and yet so effective a remedy."

The editors insert a note below his contributions:

"We wish to emphasize the last paragraph of the above. The physician should not only be thoroughly convinced that it is extremely important from a medical point of view that his patient should not become pregnant, but he should consult his conscience long and seriously before allowing himself to take a hand in this kind of business, and when he does so, the patient should not know how or where to get the preparation except through him."

Another doctor contributes to the same feature but declares his knowledge should be given freely to all who wish it. *The Medical World* responds thusly:

"to give out general information upon this subject is not to be thought of. How many men and women in your practice would shirk the duties of parenthood if they knew how, and thus miss the greatest joys of life? How many children would there be in your community if only those that are wanted would come? Far too many married people would procrastinate, saying 'No, not yet,' until the best time to procreate, or the ability to procreate had gone. Then would come a lonely old age after a desolate life. No, doctors, don't have any hand in this business."

What woman would choose motherhood if she could avoid it? I mean, women are certainly pleasant enough creatures when not under

"Ladies, to Evil!"

duress of any sort. But mentally, we can agree they're nearly indistinguishable from large sexy children who can cook. Thus women have a childlike selfishness in their capricious natures. If the cost of not having to endure bloating or back labor meant ending the human race, the average woman wouldn't think twice. Good-bye, propagation of the species, I'm keeping my twenty-eight-inch waist!

It is also possible that this publication made a point of condemning public access to birth control for the sake of legality. The Comstock Law was still in effect when this magazine was printed, though apparently with waning strictness. Insinuating that women would not be satisfied until they'd finished the destruction begun by Eve in the Garden of Eden might, I hope, have been mostly for show.

Cursing and Swearing
Is Too Tame for You Drones!

Of course some people *did* believe birth control to be one of the highest forms of selfishness and evil. Some people were authentic in their desires to populate. Some people had even done the math. Well, one person, and *some math*. That person is, of course, Mr. Fowler, in one of his finest rants.

> Till our world is full all should help fill it with the best they can; nor any refuse because they cannot have the *very* best; for poor life is as much better than none as all the happiness it can experience and impart through time and eternity.
>
> Our earth contains over 30,000,000 square miles of good arable land, with 640 acres each—about 20,000,000,000—each acre capable of clothing, housing and feeding five persons, aided by the oceans. Figure up that long string of mortals each enjoying more than tongue can tell, and all forever marching into infinitely ecstatic and everlasting bliss!
>
> What a burning shame that God's sun, air, earth, fruits, grains, and all other provisions for human enjoyments should go to waste solely because you drones are too lazy to marry or stingy to reproduce, though charring with lust! Cursing and swearing at you seems too tame. How far wrong is [it to say] that not producing is as bad as murdering that number? For who but rather exist forever yet be murdered here than not to be?"

I have no answer for his question. Partially because I...don't understand the question. One of many reasons, no doubt, the decision to reproduce should not be laid in my fumbling, feminine hands.

10

Being a Good Wife:
How to Avoid His Eventual Resentment
for as Long as Possible

NOTHING WILL INCREASE YOUR INFLUENCE,
AND SECURE YOUR USEFULNESS, MORE THAN "BEING
IN SUBJECTION TO YOUR OWN HUSBANDS."

—*William Jay*

*I*t is done. He has vowed before God and all the people he hopes to inherit money from to cherish and keep you. He can't divorce you in this era. Well, he can, but it's the modern equivalent of renting billboards all over town that show your joined families splattered in rooster blood under the words GIVE SATAN A CHANCE! So he likely won't.

But this is not the endgame. As far as nineteenth-century society is concerned, he now owns you. Your signature on any legal document is meaningless. All your property and money go under his name at the bank; you can't access them without his permission. He can beat you if he chooses, and the police won't care unless you can prove that your life is in danger. (Worse, your neighbors will tut-tut at your swollen eye, deducing that you aren't able to keep the peace in your own home.)

"That look of subjugated fear is all part of your wifely mystique."

And even though most states passed laws midcentury allowing women to at least retain their own property upon marriage, not a lot of people paid attention to them. A true woman, after all, should have no need of legal interference. A woman of wisdom and virtue can play her husband like an oboe, channeling those dopey hoot noises and flatulent squeaks into fluid melody.

So, young bride, like a tight-corseted, dainty-footed little Preakness Stakes winner, you have won the rosy wreath of triumph to wear upon your lathered brow for now, but your life's path is not determined.

Lazy days on the ranch, snout deep in oats, or off to the glue factory at the first sign of an arthritic knee?

It's all up to him. He can make your life miserable if he grows tired of you.

And he is *going* to grow tired of you.

A woman of the nineteenth century uses her youth, charm, and sexual attractiveness (of which she is supposed to be utterly un-aware) to lure a man to marry her. That way the deal is sealed before the husband learns he has fallen

THE DISSATISFIED MAN

"I have had it up to here *with your never-ending fidelity and obedience!"*

victim to a bait and switch. This blushing girl of twenty whose only joy and thought was him begins to change. Her bosoms descend to the point of looking like two oranges slapping around in the bottom of stockings, and they always have a squally little baby stuck to them. Her conversation, which used to revolve around his accomplishments and troubles, begins to include complaints and opinions of her own. Suddenly she thinks his cognac is a "luxury" but children need new shoes *every year.* Suddenly she insists a professional chimney sweep would do a better job of getting the dead pigeons out of the flue than she does. Suddenly she doesn't glow with pride while scrubbing questionable nineteenth-century hygiene out of his underwear every week.

He will not like this. And no one will be surprised if he sets out to find a new version (even if only for occasional use) of the woman who so adored him. Once again, should your neighbors catch wind of your

If you won't wear the pointy hat, he just may go find someone who will.

husband's infidelity, their glaring eyes will land on *you,* inquiring, "What did you do to drive him away, harpy?"

Your only job now that you are a nineteenth-century wife is to do everything within your power during every waking moment to make his life so sweet and full that he will literally dread the glory of Christ's return, if only because it will mean parting from your secret strudel recipe and the unmatched craftsmanship of your trouser hemstitch.

Here we explore the very worst ways a wife can offend her husband and blight her marriage.

The Most Common Paths to Marital Ruin

1. BEING MESSY

Witness "The Slovenly Wife," a tale from an 1838 edition of the ladies' periodical *The Ladies' Garland.* In it we learn the story of Hester, a girl of beauty and charm who lands a fine husband. To his dismay, he soon discovers that Hester cares about her appearance only when going out. At home she dresses indifferently. One night her sister pays an unexpected call and "was struck dumb with astonishment as she entered the room, at the embarrassment in the countenance of her brother-in-law, and the neglected appearance of his wife. [She] was dressed in her dirty, though fashionable frock, her hair partially papered, and her whole appearance gave evidence of extreme negligence." This is a description of the nineteenth-century version of an unwashed ponytail, yoga pants, and faded WILLIE NELSON HONEYSUCKLE ROSE TOUR T-shirt. Hester was chillin', unfortunately, a century and a half before it became acceptable.

Hester explains that she has no need of dressing up just to stay at home, since "her fortune is made." Her sister tries to set her straight: Hester's happiness is *not* secure. Says the sister, "Believe me, a wife's assiduous endeavors to please her husband is *[sic]* the only way to secure an interest in his affections. What can yield such a rich reward for our labors as a husband's approving smile?'"

And the real bite in the bustle? She was right. In this era, your husband is your conduit to the entire world. His pleasure dictates your well-being, as poor Hester soon learns.

She makes many a halfhearted attempt to clean up her act, but it never sticks. Her husband, too mortified to bring friends home, begins meeting with them at a nearby tavern. "From that day his flourishing business and his handsome wife became more and more neglected." Soon the husband becomes a drunkard, though he never even touched a drop before his wife's grotesque appearance drove him to the tavern. Their shop closes and they become destitute. The husband is too miserable to ever feel love for his hideous wife again. Their story closes in shame, wretchedness, and ruin.

Another life destroyed by bad fashion choices.

Formality really was a necessity. If your courtship was done respectably, you and your husband barely knew each other. It was in no one's best interest to rectify that. At least not too quickly. As coauthor J. L. Nichols reminds us in *Search Lights on Health: Light on Dark Corners,*

*Forging a new life on a wild frontier is no excuse
not to sparkle for your man.*

"Your hair was always in perfect arrangement. You never greeted him with a ragged or untidy dress or soiled hands. It is true that your 'market is made,' but you cannot afford to have it 'broken.' Cleanliness and good taste will attract now as they did formerly. Keep yourself at your best. Make the most of physical endowments."

But to be fair, Nichols was asking a lot.

It's the nineteenth century. Dust kicked up by horses coats you the second you leave your home, making a comfortable bed for all that soot and smoke in the air to lie upon. Remember, nearly every building everywhere is using some process that results in smoke and ash. Your clothing, which all but the richest ladies had to sew themselves, must be hand-washed in a soul-crushingly long process involving chemicals you have to have a permit for nowadays. Water is brought into your life by the bucketful, and darling, it is *cold*. That's just if you're in an urban area.

If you're an American farmwife, and there is, on average, a 60 percent chance that you are in this century, you'll spend your day knee deep in various dirts, animals, crops, and all the awful things that happen when you combine the three.

And pity the poor husband who comes in from the back forty to find *this* pitiful excuse for a wife waiting for him. Yes, the table is heaving with food, the cows milked, the stall mucked, the fruit preserved, and seven children bathed—but *look* at you. Just because you had to butcher a whole hog earlier this afternoon doesn't give you an excuse to look like one, dearie.

2. Getting Old

Try to understand it from his perspective: you stopped being twenty-two.

There. Do you see now? No man wants an old bat hanging around the joint, rubbing her wrinkles on the nice furniture and spreading her doughy flesh all over his bedsheets! That wasn't the deal, Grandma.

3. Asking for Stuff

American reformer William Jay, in his contemplations of the Christian marriage, tries to reason with women about their place in the grand order. He knows they *feel* like they're people, bless their hearts. But higher sources suggest otherwise.

"No, you can't have any. I said it's my *laudanum."*

"The woman is disinclined to obey, while the man is often absurd in his designs, capricious in his temper, tyrannical in his claims, and degrading in his authority. But, my sisters, while you have reason, much reason to complain, remember, it is the consequence of sin, the sin of your own sex."

And there it is, dear. You have to do what he says, and it's your own fault because for whatever reason, God smote you with the same chromosomes he gave Mother Eve, who brought sin into this world.

This might come as a shock, for in the twenty-first century you were used to equality and compromise between partners. Please adjust yourself to the following example of compromise for the duration of your stay.

Marital Compromise: Nineteenth Century

Wife: Husband, I was dearly hoping that we might call Dr. Smith regarding those recurring shooting pains my mother is experiencing in her left arm. They trouble her greatly.

Husband: Out of the question. Dr. Smith has attended my supper club and revealed himself a Democrat. We shall have no truck with his sort. Give your mother some of that German cough medicine she enjoys; that "heroin" concoction certainly lives up to its name when dealing with her!

Wife: Would you prefer lamb or brisket for supper?

If you pursue the issue further, you will be a scold or a nag. That's usually the first brick to tumble in the monument of marriage. Not to mention violating the laws of God and Nature, Little Mrs. Caused the Fall of All Mankind.

William Andrus Alcott (distant relation of known chatterbox Louisa May), in his 1837 edition of *The Young Wife, or Duties of Woman in the Marriage Relation,* devotes an entire chapter to listing the different kind of scolds that wives can become.

William Andrus Alcott just wants you to hurry up and die, nag.

The Outright Scold, who explodes in temper quick and brief. The Internal Scold, of which there are two subcategories: the woman whose unhappiness with her husband, though never spoken, is permanently on her face ("the depressed and wrinkled brow, the depressed angle of the mouth, and the peculiar turn of the sides of the nose, which indicate, that if the features have not actually grown into a scolding state, they are in great danger of it"), and the woman who occasionally forgets to keep all her anger focused quietly on her husband. This second type of Internal Scold Alcott designates an Intermittent Scold, and for her, "there is yet space for repentance and amendment of life." Blessed be.

There are even in this group, though Alcott cannot vouch for it, those who "scold most at particular periods of the moon." (The many mood-altering, madness-bringing ailments that could afflict a woman due to the particular tilt, buoyancy, or impudent mood of her womb did not at this time include premenstrual syndrome. Hysteria, however, a blanket condition describing both a woman who was having a bad week as well as one who had four husbands neatly packed in the sod beneath her root cellar, *did* exist, of course.)

Alcott offers hope. He doesn't believe a woman of this kind can be easily changed, if at all. But luckily, it's scientifically proven that scolding shortens a woman's life by decades. So, Nature will soon have

Scold's bridles, or "branks," were not used in the nineteenth century. But they were very fondly remembered in a number of historical and archaeological publications.

mercy on both her soul and yours, leaving the weary husband a great deal wiser the second time around.

Just be patient, good man. Soon the old cow will die from the pressure of her disobedient, unmet desires, and you can get a new one that doesn't talk.

In truth, women probably did nag a great deal in the nineteenth century. Nagging is a natural side effect of being powerless. If a lady *could* withdraw money from her husband's account, pay calls until she locates a trustworthy handyman, and have the shingles on the roof repaired without bothering her husband, she would. If she *could* get a part-time job to pay for her own needs without announcing to the entire community that her husband is a bum who can't provide for his children and ungrateful wife, she would. But she can't do any of that. So she must wheedle and remind and even beg. Right into the grave.

4. HAVING OPINIONS, PASSIONS, AND STRENGTHS

Are you an operatic soprano with perfect pitch? Little lady, you just made front row in the church choir.

Mind teeming with complex plots aching to be shaped in beautiful language?
Ooh, the little ones will love that at bedtime!

Impeccable at math and bookkeep-
ing? You—best keep that to yourself. Just
keep a tidy budget for the household, and
if someone asks your opinion of current
stock-market prices, say you don't raise
cows but your milk deliveries have been
reasonable.

For the average man, no worldly
knowledge, talent, or strength in a woman
will make her a better wife. Not here.

*"I'm sorry. I thought I was reading
my newspaper, yet it seems you're
still talking at me. One of us must
be making a mistake."*

Nichols explains, "However much
men may admire the public performance of gifted women, they do not
desire that boldness and dash in a wife. The holy blush of a maiden's
modesty is more powerful in hallowing and governing a home than the
heaviest armament that ever a warrior bore."

Simply put, gifted women would have other interests besides home
and husband. No, thank you. This, he continues, is what makes a good
wife:

"A woman to be the best home maker needs to be devoid of intensive 'nerves.' She must be neat and systematic, but not too neat, lest she destroy the comfort she endeavors to create. She must be distinctly amiable, while firm. She should have no 'career,' or desire for a career, if she would fill to perfection the home sphere.... She must be affectionate, sympathetic and patient, and fully appreciative of the worth and dignity of her sphere."

Nearly every author of this era does encourage a wife to keep a keen and healthy mind, however. Especially by reading her husband's newspapers and learning about the machinations of his particular line of work. Because some nights he'll be bored and might talk to you. You need to be ready!

Don't overdo it, of course. The point is to charm and relax your husband. You provide the attractive parsley garnish to his conversa-

The way a man likes to see his wife gaining knowledge.
Bonus points if the pages are blank.

tional meal. Useless, but he'll appreciate the effort. It isn't your job to upstage him with your own views and interests. If you open dinner conversation with your opinions on how the Second Opium War will end up affecting the Qing dynasty, you best be speaking to a member of the Qing dynasty. Whose wives were not exactly known for expressing themselves either, by the way.

5. Being a Bad Cook

The key to being a good wife appears to be an assemblage of things you *don't* do. You don't express need, you don't express ideas, you show no hurt, and generally you function as a well-groomed iron girder, supporting the architecture of your husband's life. There is one area, however, where your husband requires you to be active and enthusiastic, authoritative even. Not in the bedroom. That's...that's just disgusting. And you're disgusting for thinking it. No! In the *kitchen*.

Meals in this era are an arduous undertaking, very unlike what you were used to in the twenty-first century. The food you eat either has to be coaxed from the earth through primitive and unreliable farming methods, or chased down, subdued, and killed before you can eat it. You can buy food in a store; canned foods started to become available early midcentury in America. But there is no FDA, no sanitation standards, and Louis Pasteur won't show the world how to kill off bacteria through heat until 1864. And when he does, not everyone will listen to him. Ketchups are tinted with rust to make them red, bakers increase the weight of their bread loaves with chalk and grit, and with no refrigeration or pesticides, *everything* is one hot breath away from spoilage. So as depressed as we might have been microwaving ourselves a paper towel's worth of chicken nuggets for dinner, that's vastly preferable to the chance you take in sitting down to a meal in the nineteenth century.

Tonight's menu? Unless you are excruciatingly careful and sometimes even if you are, look forward to intestinal worms, lead poisoning, and four-day-old unrefrigerated pork with a side of botulism.

So the authors who stressed that a good wife had to be a good cook or, if she be wealthy enough, educated on the art of cooking so as to oversee her employees, weren't *just* being pedantic. They feared "dyspepsia," which encompassed all digestive troubles that didn't prove fatal. A wife's job was to prevent that. Pye Henry Chavasse, who was not only a doctor but also named after an actual food (either fact being enough to qualify him as an expert), sermonizes at length on the issue in his *Advice to a Wife on the Management of Her Own Health:*

> "Do not think that I am overstating the importance of my subject. A good dinner—I mean a well-cooked dinner (which, be it ever so plain, is really a good dinner)—is absolutely essential to the health, to the very existence of yourself and your husband; and how, if it be left to the tender mercies of the present race of cooks, can you have it? High time it is that every wife, let her station be either high or low, should look into the matter herself, and remedy the crying evil of the day."

Of course the reasonable proposal that a woman oversee the production of nonpoisonous food in her home begins to go off the rails a bit. The nineteenth-century thinkers never seem happy with "reason" unless there's a tipple of shame poured over it, too. And Chavasse has a flair for shame.

> "I will, moreover, maintain that no man can be a thorough-

ly good man who has a bad cook—it is an utter impossibility! A man who partakes of a badly-cooked dinner is sure, as I have just now remarked, to be dyspeptic, and, if dyspeptic, to be quarrelsome, snappish, and unamiable, the one following the other as a matter of course. Take warning, therefore, O ye wives! and look to the dinners of your husbands, and know yourselves how dinners ought to be cooked!"

One more way to drive your husband to ruin, to taverns, to strumpets. And don't think serving a well-cooked meal is the extent of your duty, O ye wives. We

Dyspepsia: destroyer of lives, destroyer of wives.

use (hand-sew, hand-wash, and bleach daily) *tablecloths* in this house, madam. And echhh! I hate it when my dumplings are touching my greens! You know I hate that!

As a writer named William Martin—who appropriated the name and gender of "Old Chatty (Charlotte) Cheerful!" to write this 1861 missive—reminds us, it is detail and civility that separate us from swine.

> "Yet how many bad housewives are there who never have their husbands' meals ready at the proper time. A man who has perhaps only half-an-hour to eat his breakfast in, can't afford to wait. If he have to wait, he must do it at the loss of temper, and loss of temper involves loss of appetite, and sometimes loss of peace for

the whole day. Then, again, how frequently have I seen a work-ing man sitting down to his breakfast or dinner without a bit of cloth on the table, with dirty knives and forks, dirty salt in a dirty salt-cellar; pork, dumplings, greens, and potatoes, all muddled into one dish, and the whole without order or cleanliness; badly cooked, and so wretchedly served as to look disgusting. Then the man sits down, all in a broil, perhaps; the woman all in a broil, from her cooking; the children all in a broil, and dirty from the streets, where they have been playing, none of them washed, but all with dirty hands and dirty faces, gather together, like so many pigs, to eat the food God has given them."

What excuses can this poor woman give for failing to properly stage her husband's meal? Teething babies, difficult interactions with servants, slow loss of mobility due to rickets—the reasons exist. But it just didn't matter. A slice of burnt toast in the morning could trigger a terrifying series of events. It makes one wonder how many lives might have been spared if just one of Genghis Khan's concubines had known her way around a kitchen.

6. Getting Mad When He Cheats

Well, here you are. You didn't know each other to begin with, turns out five kids later you still haven't really hit it off, and now you, the wife, have gone all puffy and talk too much. So…he's gonna duck out for a quick pick-me-up now and then.

Now, you can go all "my womb is enraged and I shall visit the wrath of it upon you" when your husband cheats (which is just *so* like a woman!) or you can go super-classy. Alexander Walker, in his 1840 *Woman Physiologically Considered, as to Mind, Morals, Marriage,*

The proper thing to do here is make your apologies
and let him know the Petersons are coming for dinner.
Then leave; the man is obviously busy.

Matrimonial Slavery, Infidelity and Divorce, tells the story of a well-to-do lady who discovered her husband was keeping a lover. She found that the girl, who was poor and easily seduced, was being kept in a shabby apartment. So she arranged to have it nicely furnished, as befitting her husband's taste. When he realized what his clever wife had done, he confronted her. Instead of giving him a scolding, she replied "that such was her affection for him, that she loved him in all places, and was desirous of doing anything for his convenience, credit and comfort." This of course brought the man to his senses, and he left his plaything to return to the arms of his wise and loving wife, who was such a class act that she even arranged a small annuity to support the girl he'd ruined.

Ladies, that is what you do with a cheating husband.

Walker says, "How much more commendable was the behavior of these women than that of those who rail at their imprudent or incontinent husbands, and by their conduct render that home which before was undesirable, quite hateful and insupportable!" That is to say, if he didn't want to hang around you before you developed a martyr complex, how appealing must he find you now?

Besides, Walker reminds us, caring more about your husband's happiness than your own isn't just prudent, it's biblical. Godly heroines like Sarah, Leah, and Rachel all gave the most beautiful of their maids up for their husbands' use.

Just like you will.

Sarah and her maid Hagar. Spoiler: it didn't end great for Hagar.

And not just because it's good manners to share your husband's vitality; it's also the safest option for you if your man has a wandering eye. If you, the wife, allow him one clean, pretty little plaything, he won't have to sneak around with larger numbers of lesser women. After all, it was in the mid-nineteenth century that the world of promiscuity and extramarital sex took a big turn for the ugly. Seeping-sores, horrible-pox, and slow-nerve-failure ugly.

Why the huge uptick in sexually transmitted diseases? It was the factories, if you can believe it! With the Industrial Revolution under way, for the first time young men and women realized they didn't *have* to spend the rest of their lives staring at a cow's pungent hind end. They went to the cities to work in manufacturing, shipping, and hospitality industries.

For our purposes here, we're going to file prostitution under hospitality industries. Business boomed. For the most part, Victorian ladies of all but the lowest classes still kept their virtue tightly intact, so men were not able to relieve what they'd been taught were unhealthy buildups with that particular population. It was the women who had the misfortune to be born into starvation, filth, and poverty who filled this need. The strumpet, the streetwalker, our fallen sisters, the painted ladies, the women of the evening, the soiled doves. Prostitutes.

Prostitution of the olden days is glamorized today. Sultry, sassy brothels filled with velvet and laughter—you had to be quite attractive and young to get into one of those, and then all your earnings belonged to your pimp or madam. Plus you were out on your unmarriageable, unemployable bottom once your looks faded. Most urban prostitutes spent their nights leaning against the same freezing alley walls, being used as little more than public trash receptacles. Few made it to age forty.

Disease was almost a given. And if your beloved husband

THE GREAT SOCIAL EVIL.

The carefree life of a Victorian prostitute

brought it back to you, your life, home, and marriage would be devastated. Forgetting your own immense discomfort and the congenital defects of children you might conceive, there was the fact that a lot of doctors wouldn't want to upset your delicate lady-brain by telling you what you actually *had*.

In his 1904 treatise *Social Diseases and Marriage: Social Prophylaxis,* Prince (a name, not a title) Albert Morrow debated the question of whether to tell a wife that her husband's infidelity had resulted in a painful, possibly incurable infection.

> "The fixed rule of professional conduct in these cases, from which there can be no deviation, is that no information or hint even of the nature of the disease should come from the physician....
>
> It is a question whether it is better in the interest of the wife as well as of the husband that she should not know or even suspect the nature of her disease, if it can be possibly concealed from her, and thus spare her the mental anguish, the sense of injury, shame, and humiliation which would come from the revelation."

Syphilitic pustules spread to the face

By comparison, men believing that you are too weak to own property or vote doesn't seem nearly as insulting, does it? Your burning and blistered genitals? Oh, madam, tut-tut.

We do not talk about such things in polite company or in my medical exam room. Now, keep injecting your unspeakable region with this iodine and mercury sublimate until I tell you to stop. *Because I said so, that's why!*

Morrow doesn't completely support this silence, because he doesn't believe women are dim enough to fall for it. Which is generous of him, because a particularly slow-witted monkey wouldn't be dim enough to fall for it.

Cocaine wine: one lovely option for coping with your new position as a nineteenth-century wife.

"Notwithstanding the most painstaking precautions on the part of the physician in concealing the character of the remedies employed, the exercise of his diplomacy in parrying her embarrassing questions as to 'why she should have the same symptoms as her husband,' etc., and in persuading her of the necessity of continuing treatment in the absence of all manifestations, sooner or later she is apt to divine the nature of the disease for which she is treated, so that the little comedy of deception and falsehood most often proves a dismal failure."

And then she'll be diseased *and* quite irritated. Bad news all around, madam: it turns out that the doctor has diagnosed you with stupidity as well as syphilis.

No, the best course of action to take if you suspect your husband of "infelicity" is to make the experience as pleasing for him as possible. J. L. Nichols offers this analogy:

"He has his peculiarities. He has no right to many of them, and you need to know them; thus you can avoid many hours of friction. The good pilot steers around the sunken rocks that lie in the channel. The engineer may remove them, not the pilot. You are more pilot than engineer. Consult his tastes. It is more important to your home that you should please him, than anybody else."

And you better believe that includes yourself.

Running a Proper Household:
The Gentle Art of Dictatorship

*W*ithout other compelling distractions, the wealthy and educated have spent a great deal of time thinking up rules. Instincts are no longer to be trusted, and the simplest way is by no means the best anymore. Even something as straightforward as inviting a guest to come inside your home is a heady undertaking fraught with potential faux pas. You cannot simply say, "Come in, have a seat." A guest will be lost with a command as vague as that. What seat? What room? May the guest enter unaccompanied, or is it the current fashion that she bring an elderly Albanian man as an escort? The Albanian—shall he use a simple brass filigreed walking stick, or does the season call for a bamboo cane? A good hostess leaves no room for confusion.

Parlor. Definitely a parlor. Unless it's the drawing room.

The Honor Corner and the Distant Seat of Manliness

Tonight, darling, is the night you prove your worth as a wife, nay, a *woman* to all the people whose opinion matter. Family and friends? No! *Cherie,* will you *pay attention!* I swear I would rap your fine knuckles with my fan if you were before me! You're a woman of Victorian society, and your singular goal is to increase your standing in that society. It's not just about snootiness either. You do this for your family's well-being. Pleasing and befriending the wives of his superiors will elevate your husband in his career. As well as for your children, whose futures rest on recommendations from the right people and good marriage matches.

Your guests are arriving. Now, go stand in an attitude of grace and hospitality mixed with a reserved regal bearing and wait in the hall!

That is most certainly a parlor. Wait...no. That wallpaper just screams drawing room. Maybe it's the sitting room?

Get your expression set straight. You're pleased to see them, but not excited. Smile smaller. No teeth, you little badger! *Smaller.* There!

In the interest of time, we will restrict ourselves to the rules of attending to guests as explained by a single author, unnamed, writing in 1840 in the book *Etiquette for Ladies: With Hints on the Preservation, Improvement, and Display of Female Beauty.* But be aware, there were as many versions of the following danse macabre as there are stars in the sky.

First of all, your visitor shall be invited into the drawing room, not the parlor. (I am sure there is a difference, though what it is presently escapes me.) Unless you are too poor to afford a drawing room, in which case the parlor must do. Unless you are too poor to afford a parlor, in which case you probably don't need a book of this nature. Wouldn't your pennies be better spent procuring butcher's scraps to fortify your pottage? But if you insist, you may receive the guest in the dining room, which otherwise is to be avoided. And if your financial means only allows you to crowd your guests into your dining area, please behave in a manner appropriate to your glaring poverty: don't throw lavish affairs that will embarrass everyone because they suspect you must be sending your seven-year-old out to work as a chimney sweep in order to pay for them.

Mrs. Pettibone has very strong ideas about what Miss Whipp did to warrant possession of the only armchair, and they are not charitable.

Now, positioning the guests.

A young man: Offer him an armchair or a stuffed chair.

An elderly man: Insist he take the armchair.

A lady: Beg her to be seated on the sofa.

More than one lady: Give the nicest chair to the most important one. (This might be the eldest, but not in every case. Wealth, social position, and general mastery of feminine warfare also qualify.)

In winter: Place the nicest chair at the corner of the fireplace. This is considered the most honorable seat in the house. The farther you are from the fireplace, the lower your social rank.

A married lady, in winter: Take her by the hand and conduct her to the corner of the fireplace.

If a gentleman is host: Seat guests, then place a chair at a distance from the guests. Sit there. This is either to avoid intimidating those who trespass on your generosity or to increase intimidation.

If a lady is hostess to an intimate friend: She may sit next to her on the sofa, which is where you will remember a lady is to be sat unless she is married, because then she must go to the Corner of Honor.

If a lady is hostess to multiple ladies: She will form a horseshoe of furniture and take a chair at the center of it.

If you roll five of a kind: This is considered Yahtzee, and you may demand the Corner of Honor whether it be winter or summer, unless the chair has arms *and* is stuffed; then you lose a turn.

As you can see, even this very small piece of domestic life is an absolute spider's web of propriety. You can either be the one who deftly creates it, like the deadly *Atrax robustus* spinning her swirling vortex of terrifying delicacy, or you can be one of the small hapless frogs that stumble into it, your clumsy vibrations heralding your doom.

We can't possibly cover every aspect of keeping a worthy Victorian home, for reasons you'll discover later. But we can touch on some of the interactions you'll be expected to navigate, particularly involving the many nonfamily people who will be in your home.

Helping Servants Remember
They Are Appreciated—Pieces of Furniture

"You tend to your second-degree burns on your own time, missy."

Good news. As we have decided you are wealthy, because you sure as cesspits don't want to be anywhere near this century if you are not, there is a great deal of work in your household that you won't actually have to do. You have "domestics." In this era even a middle-class family would employ at least one maid-of-all-work to keep a household running and, if finances allowed, a cook, since cooking anything beyond porridge and stews was an all-day affair. Then, depending on the size of your home and estate, your next acquisition would likely be a man-of-all-work, to do handyman deeds (for at this point the man of the house must be putting in very long hours on his job or mistress) and heavy lifting.

Servants like these did not indicate ridiculous wealth. Even with a cook and a maid, the average woman's day would still be filled with a degree and kind of labor that even the most high-performing woman of today would find unbearably vexatious. A good nineteenth-century housewife was a dedicated and hardworking micromanager.

Besides supervising the care and education of her children (public schools were neither universally available nor compulsory in America until the twentieth century), she had a complicated household economy to oversee. Everything we get at the grocery store had to be purchased from separate vendors on separate accounts. She had to stay in communication with the dairy, the butcher, the dry-goods store, and the "grocery," where fresh fruit and vegetables were purchased. Then there were the clothing and household

In middle-class houses, the maid will clean up the spilled coal, but the spankin' is still all Mama's job.

items that she likely had to make and maintain by herself for her family (for a middle-class family, if a seamstress or tailor was employed, it would be for a single "best" dress or suit of clothing). For the vast majority of the families that employed them, servants did the broad, heavy work, things we seldom do today at all. The maid might scrub the floor and sweep the ashes out of the fireplace, thank heavens, but that simply freed up the wife to get down on *her* knees and spot-clean the upholstery on her parlor furniture with a special cleansing concoction her own mother taught her. That said, even the kindest mistress was a *mistress*, not a friend and not an equal to her servants. And if she was an unkind mistress, she would work extra diligently to make sure the servants were constantly aware of their inferiority, as we shall see.

For wealthy families like yours (yes, yes, you're welcome), household labor was apportioned much more precisely. Scullery maids, housemaids, underhousemaids, laundry maids, chef, cook, confectioner, pastry cook, steward's boy, valet, groom, valet-groom, and hall usher—the procession of help was endless. And no, the mistress of the house did not spot-clean her own upholstery. She would have the chair sent out to its designer for repair. The mistress would not even have to balance her own accounts; that's what a trusted housekeeper (the highest female position in a grand house) did. Often there would be less struggle between master and servant in the larger houses. The servants would likely be paid more and have more fellow workers to help shoulder the workload. Plus there was pride in being employed by a large estate.

Some of the servants these folks kept were just ridiculous. What does a hall usher even do? But most were truly required to keep large houses and important people functioning. As fey and snooty as it all seems to us, social events were quite important then, one of the few opportunities people had to interact and judge one another's characters. If a man wanted to advance in the world, he truly did need his wife at

"Our lives of inglorious servitude will one day be dramatized to entertain and delude millions."

his side at parties, well turned out and charming, to show prospective business and social contacts that he was a man of good taste and comfortable means. A wife couldn't play the role of impressive ornament for him if she was busy cleaning and cooking for a crowd.

We still have domestic help in the twenty-first century. It's not unheard of for even middle-class families to have a "Manuel, he does such a great job with roses, I'd be living in a hollowed-out briar patch without that guy" or a "Katya, she comes and helps clean the house out every two weeks. We'd *die* without her!" The wealthy add nannies, tutors, personal fitness coaches. But we're much less likely to acknowledge any difference in class between helper and helped, at least overtly. Class delineation makes us uncomfortable. We have a core belief in our time that any honest worker is worthy of respect, usually more than those who have inherited wealth.

That's a very new thing, and very American. The nineteenth century marked the beginning of the end of the immemorial belief that one person could be superior to another simply by virtue of their bloodline. If William the Conqueror bequeathed a large chunk of land to a favored knight (who himself could not have attained the rank of knight without money backing him), for the next nine hundred years that knight's descendants would live without laboring, collecting large dividends and rents from the peasants who paid them to use and inhabit that estate. The wars of the twentieth century would bleed England and other European powers white, cut off their empires, and demand wealth redistribution that would make even the most liberal American blanch. But that hasn't happened yet. You in the nineteenth century are witness to the fading but still-glorious sunset of domestic servitude.

In America, things were...messier. Particularly in the South, where instead of domestic servants, people had house slaves, who were

*It reads: "These poor creatures are a sacred legacy from
my ancestors and while a dollar is left me, nothing shall be spared
to increase their comfort and happiness." Behold the giant,
joy-filled family picnic that was slavery.*

either already holding, or on the way to holding, the highest rank available to them. Being of personal service to his or her owner was as far
away from the unspeakable misery of the fields as a slave could hope to

be. Sometimes, due to the length of time master and slave had known each other and the intimacy in which they lived, the relationship bordered on familial. But in a sickly, degrading way.

I presume that, however beguiling the grandeur of Scarlett O'Hara's Technicolor world seems to you, however happy the well-fed, shiny-faced Mammy seems in devoting her life to helping her ungrateful owners thrive, the slave-holding South is one place you don't want to visit. So we will leave it in history, where it belongs.

In the American North, nineteenth-century maids and footmen didn't have to fear being sold away from their children or beaten for being slow. Plus, they were actual free Americans, in a culture that never was and never would be entirely comfortable with unyielding servitude. Unlike in England, where being a servant was a lifelong profession, American servants were always ready for something better to come along, be it marriage or a chance to work in their cousin's store. So securing good service from them could be a chore. In fact, servants and those who thought they deserved round-the-clock service (a privilege usually afforded only to babies, the enfeebled, and people who rule nations and occasionally sign execution orders) clashed all the time.

Therefore, a proper nineteenth-century mistress treats her servants with firm benevolence. However, according to *Etiquette for Ladies,* you must never:

- Allow them to appear in your presence looking "too slatternly or too finely dressed." A servant who is "too finely dressed" must be dangerously close to considering herself just as human as her mistress.
- Allow them to "answer you by signs or coarse terms." (Signs

include nodding; "coarse terms" would be using the word "yes" without "miss" following it.)

- Allow them to enter into conversation with each other in your presence.
- Scold your servants. They are not children. Children get second chances. No, it is preferable to "turn them away at once." There will always be another girl waiting on the back stoop who prefers grueling labor and being treated like furniture to a life of starvation or prostitution.

"Go be adorably feisty somewhere else, you Irish ragamuffin."

As for dismissing servants, unless they do something very bad, you have to give them notice, usually a month, during which time they may try to procure a new place. A new place, especially in the same field of work, is near impossible to find without references—that is, at least one letter from a previous employer vouching for a servant's honesty and ability. Thomas Hill, a prolific and respected writer of guidebooks on everything from thanking a railway conductor to writing succinct and tasteful tombstone inscriptions, offers an example in one of his etiquette books of how to end a woman's career, possibly her ability to support herself (note the name of the servant—it's those Irish thugs again!):

"Mrs. Ballard:

In reply to your note of enquiry, I decline to recommend Bridget Mallory. She is both dishonest and addicted to intemperance."

Even worse is to be dismissed "summarily," or immediately, for one of the following infractions, detailed in 1873's *Cassell's Household Guide,* volume 1:

"When a domestic servant is guilty of immoral conduct, willfully refuses to obey orders, gets intoxicated, stays out all night without being able to give a satisfactory reason for so doing, or habitually neglects to carry out his or her master's (or mistress's) lawful commands, such domestic servant may be summarily dismissed, without any more wages being paid than are actually due. Of course in cases of detected theft...master or mistress has the right to cause the servants' rooms and boxes to be examined."

You may be a forty-five-year-old woman, but if you live under *my* Queen Anne off-center dormers protruding fashionably from a steeply gabled roof, you live by *my* rules. A servant is basically like a teenager with endless chores, except that teenagers usually have car privileges and even if such a thing existed, no lower-class Victorian housemaid would even be allowed to polish the chrome. Because she'd probably rip it right off and sell it to indulge in whiskey and games of chance.

All hail the washing machine, off-the-rack clothes, faster transportation of goods, electric appliances, and every other time-saving device that will flood the markets of the early twentieth century, setting those who wish it, free of the two-way tyranny of servitude.

Ah, but we are not there yet. You still must use all your finesse to keep your domestics working well, without letting them feel as if they could do any better.

Most of all, no matter what hour of this fading dusk of service you live in, be wary of how you treat servants in front of distinguished company. Nothing so declares a woman of low class than her needing to make an effort to appear superior to servants. Take it from John A. Ruth and S. L. Louis, the authors of 1882's *Decorum: A Practical Treatise on Etiquette and Dress of the Best American Society:*

> "If you ask the waiter for anything, you will be careful to speak to him gently in the tone of request, and not of command. To speak to a waiter in a driving manner will create, among well-bred people, the suspicion that you were sometime a servant yourself, and are putting on airs at the thought of your promotion."

Having servants really could be quite a headache, dear, though you would not know it from the stories you've most enjoyed. But the unsurprising fact is, people preferred servitude only to starving or freezing to death. That was it. And if that's all you're offering, you can't expect much in return.

Dinner: The Final Reckoning

Headache or not, the pinnacle of nineteenth-century domestic society is the dinner party, and it cannot be done without servants. It can't be done without a lot of things, actually. But here is one thing you can do away with right now, before we even select the menu: practicality.

In the twenty-first century, even the starchiest of homes usually enforced only the most basic table manners. With the exception of the arbitrary "Elbows off the table" edict, those manners were common-sense interpretations of "Don't be gross" and "Share." But the nineteenth century is different; it is a time of ceremony and romance. Two things that seldom occupy the same space as common sense.

I do not know what it feels like, after years of study and observation, to suddenly be thrust for the first time into the middle of an inner-city emergency room where lives hang on your ability to remember the procedures you've learned. But I'm almost certain it wouldn't be as complicated or nerve-racking as your first formal nineteenth-century dinner.

Breakfast, tea, and luncheon all have their own rules. (And do please remember, only a leather-skinned fishwife refers to luncheon as "dinner," or dinner as "supper.") But dinner is the ultimate test of your domestic etiquette, so we will focus on it.

Your guests should be assembled in your most guestly room at the correct time (see above), and you with them. Their number should be, as the adage of the day goes, "more than the Graces (three) and less than the Muses (nine)." Really, though, guests numbering up to twelve are acceptable. Thirteen are not. We know thirteen is not a wicked number, but it is still widely believed that if you eat thirteen to a meal, one of the company will die within the year. Of course it is a superstition, but at this point, so is sterilizing wounds with alcohol. You can't pick and choose.

A domestic shall announce the serving of dinner. And not scrubby little Colleen from the kitchen with her insipid Irish sputter. Oh, pish. That's not racist. It's factual. *No one* likes the Irish in this century, brutish sots. Their time will come; we'll get all gooey for them for most of the twentieth century and beyond. But for now, your (English if possible) butler, at his most rigid, is preferred for this task.

Seating arrangements are to have been set out beforehand. You are to have planned this seating with no less attention than you would give to an international summit between warring nations. Which is quite likely what you're doing, on a small scale. Mrs. Pettibone next to Miss Whipp? Do not think that just because two years have passed that Miss Whipp has forgotten Mrs. Pettibone's withering jabs about the neckline of her summer gown at the Clydespark Promenade. And Mrs. Pettibone is not going to apologize; she feels she did Miss Whipp a service to keep her from further embarrassing herself, and if you want to know why Miss Whipp is entering her fourth social season and *still* no marriage proposals, just ask Mrs.—oh, just put them far away from each other, dear.

Also remember to avoid seating together two people who like each other a great deal, or even two people who share an occupation. Because they might talk to each other, separate from the whole of the party, about things they find interesting. And if everyone *else* has to spend three hours discussing floral displays at the city park and which Swiss

Place the most attractive guests in a position of easy access to the lecherous. We're all here to have fun.

finishing school does the best job of sterilizing a daughter into scalding purity, so do they.

As host, offer second helpings of every course. As a guest, never, ever accept this invitation. The preparation, presentation, and consumption of this meal are as carefully timed as a space-shuttle launch; your deciding you simply *must* have another go at those asparagus spears can derail the whole process.

The properly set table varies in this century depending on the etiquette book you read. But at the height of the Victorian period, the finest of table settings will provide at least four forks, two knives, and one spoon, and three plates and four glasses. A similar version is described by Robert Tomes in *The Bazar Book of Decorum:*

"To the right of the soup plate will be four glasses, tumbler first, then the Madeira, then the claret, and finally the Champagne

Reproduction of a full Victorian dinner service.
Many of these utensils were used only for serving. Choose wisely.

glass. Two large knives and forks are placed with the knives on the right and forks on the left of each guest; and when the dessert is to be eaten, a silver knife and fork and spoon are served upon the small plate, with the finger-bowl and doily. The guest, on receiving these, spreads his doily on his left, deposits the finger-bowl upon it, and noiselessly sets his knife on the right and his fork and spoon on the left."

Are you taking notes?

Mrs. Beeton's Bill of Fare

Mrs. Isabella Beeton,
shortly before her death

The table is set; now, what will you serve? Let's ask Mrs. Isabella Beeton, authoress of the exhaustive and best-selling 1861 *Beeton's Book of Household Management.* Beeton was the industrious young wife of a magazine publisher, eldest of twenty-one children, and not a particular expert in any of the many subjects she advised upon, which ranged from how to pick the tastiest breed of sheep straight from the field to the art of administering a turpentine enema. Her authoritative tone and the sheer volume of her words disguised her inexperience. She wrote *Household Management* in her early twenties, borrowing liberally (plagiarizing, but no one really cared) from many other cookbooks and etiquette books. Sadly, Beeton did not live to see the long-lasting success of her work. After suffering many miscarriages and losing two of her four children in infancy, she died of childbirth (puerperal) fever at age twenty-eight. Her biographers believe her husband's syphilis might have been a factor in her miscarriages and death.

Her work remains one of the clearest windows into (ideal) Victorian culture, evidenced in the following "Bill of Fare," given as an example of a proper October dinner for twelve persons.

Oh! One last thing before service. Never allow your waiters to serve from the right. A person of good breeding will not have been allowed to achieve maturity with the sinister hand dominant, or, as we say today, left-handed. (India ink dripping from the nib of a pen did not dry fast enough to prevent a trailing left hand from making every epistle a smear.) Therefore it is far more convenient for all guests to serve themselves from the proffered dishes if they are reaching to the left with their stronger right hand. And they *do* serve themselves. This isn't a military mess hall where sweaty men slap ladles of pungent mush on your plate. No. Your pungent mush will be offered delicately by trained servants wielding precise mush-serving utensils.

First Course

Soup: *Soup à la Crecy (Carrot Soup), Soup à la Reine.* Never decline the soup, even if you don't plan to eat it. You'll look pathetic being the only one with an empty plate, and that makes people uncomfortable.

Fish: *Baked Cod, Stewed Eels.* (The fish course may be declined.) Use a fish fork unless the host is too poor to have fish forks. Then just use one of the other four forks you ought to have been provided. Not that one. No, *that* one is specifically for oysters, which really, *cherie,* is something any adolescent schoolboy would know. Try the small one toward the outside of the line.

Hors d'oeuvres: Such as olives, radishes, or anchovy salads. Oh, yes, they are *so* a viable salad base. "Salad" has taken on a very narrow meaning during your lifetime, one that you must now expand. Eat your pickled stink-fish.

ENTREES COURSE

Ris de Veau and Tomato Sauce, Pork Cutlets and Sauce Robert, Vol-au-Vent of Chicken, Grilled Mushrooms. These are also called the side dishes, and you must use only your fork to eat them. Probably the bigger one. All right, I honestly don't know which one. But it's possible that no one actually does. If anyone questions you, say you picked up the habit of using this particular fork during your time at the Sorbonne and have had trouble shaking it.

Also, don't keep your knife clutched like a dagger in your hand as you eat. It looks utterly primitive. If you must cut a hard substance into bitable size, do so in small portions and then retire the knife.

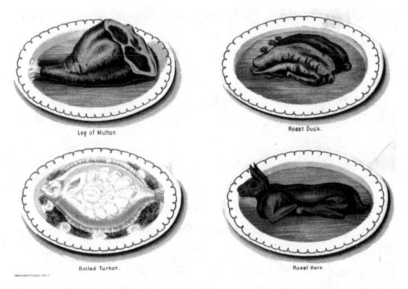

Leg of Mutton.

Roast Duck.

Boiled Turbot.

Roast Hare.

Request that the heads be left on whenever possible. It's more classy.

SECOND COURSE

Rump of Beef à la Jardinière, Roast Goose, Boiled Fowls in Celery Sauce, Tongue That Has Been Garnished, Vegetables. This is the heaviest meat-and-vegetable course. As livestock farming hasn't reached the astounding production we're familiar with today, be prepared for more birds, fish, small game, and tongue pieces than you're used to. If your favorite bit of the garnished tongue happens to be the esophagus end, it is impolite to request it. This probably won't be an issue. Regarding vegetables: they will be boiled. Like someone filled a silicone carrot mold of a fake carrot with Gerber vegetable mush. Eat them and be glad that the process of destroying this perfectly good vegetable probably killed a great deal of parasites.

THIRD COURSE

Grouse, Pheasants, Quince Jelly, Lemon Cream, Apple Tart, Compote of Peaches, Nesselrode Pudding, Cabinet Pudding, Scalloped Oysters: This course provides an array of sweet dishes, hot pudding, and slow-moving birds.

DESSERT AND ICES COURSE

Mrs. Beeton doesn't specify the dessert menu to complement this particular meal, but desserts in this century commonly consist of cheeses, fruit, cakes, sweetmeats (nuts), and sorbetlike ices. Coffee and liqueur usually follow. As with all courses, never hesitate to take the last piece or serving of any dessert if offered. Declining such an offer, which you might consider a polite gesture, is actually a declaration to your host that you noticed he has no official drawing room and is probably too poor to spare the food.

At this point you might be wishing you'd time-traveled to ancient Rome, where feasts were just as varied and ample, but a good host would provide long feathers to help his guests vomit when they were full, that they might continue merrymaking. Victorians are seldom so practical.

It is a long-held tradition that after the meal has concluded the sexes separate. The ladies go to the "withdrawing room," or, as we know it, the drawing room, so that they may gossip and twaddle while the men smoke foul tobacco, pour heavy liquors, and tell lascivious stories about Frenchwomen. However, there are many homes in this health-minded era where men of breeding getting sloppy drunk is frowned upon. So the sexes often retire together, as women of equally good breeding have the ability to suck all the masculinity and merriment out of an occasion. After an hour of stiff socializing, your guests will finally take their gracious leave.

Paring Pears for Pairs

The rules set forth in this chapter may seem entirely arbitrary and largely lacking the soul of politeness, which is simply to show kindness to those around you. The uncompromising seating arrangement that allows the richest guest the nicest chair does not seem the best way to keep joy and gentleness flowing at a party.

Honestly, I believe these rules were a sort of test. Throughout history, a man's whole wealth, future, and lifestyle (and that of his ancestors) could be known at a glance. There were even laws in some parts of Europe that forbade common people from dressing as nicely as the nobility. But the innovations, wars, and social upheavals of the late eighteenth and nineteenth centuries changed all that. Suddenly the orphan son of a prostitute could grow up to own steel empires while a seventh-generation duke could find himself penniless because he had no idea how to use his land beyond allowing peasants to work it for him.

So people made rules. Hard, insidious little rules, which you could really learn only through a lifetime of observation and practice. That way, the duke was still a gentleman, but the steel baron would show himself to be one of the upstarts, the rough and tactless nouveaux riches.

Therefore, these rules are important. These rules are righteous. Everyone needs to play by these rules! You can almost hear the gritted teeth through which the authors Ruth and Louis allow that Queen Victoria herself has strayed from them:

HER MAJESTY'S GRACIOUS SMILE.

> "Queen Victoria has set the fashion of placing the whole loaf of bread upon the table with a knife by its side, leaving the bread to be cut as it is desired. However, the old style of having the bread already cut when it is placed upon the table will still recommend itself to many."

Her Majesty will eat her bread with a rusty garden trowel if she so chooses, thereby making the practice Victorian. So suck it.

One mustn't suggest Her Royal Highness is indulging in a boorish abuse of simple, sacred etiquette, even if she is. Just think of the crumbs that will fall as each piece is whacked and sawed by people entirely too refined to ever have been trained in the lower arts, like barrel making or bread slicing.

I fear I simply cannot supply you with all the information you will need to properly run a socially keen home; there is just too much. Still, let me leave you with some choice hints from Messrs. Ruth and Louis:

Socializing is mandatory. After all, there are crazy cat ladies in every century, and you don't want to be counted among them.

"Never pare an apple or a pear for a lady unless she desire you, and then be careful to use your fork to hold it; you may sometimes offer to divide a very large pear with or for a person.

Cheese must be eaten with a fork.

Never lay your hand or play with your fingers upon the table. Neither toy with your knife, fork or spoon, make pills of your bread nor draw imaginary lines upon the table-cloth.

Never bite fruit. An apple, pear or peach should be peeled with a silver knife, and all fruit should be broken or cut."

Never bite fruit. That's what we're dealing with, inside your own *home,* my gosling. No, you can't lock yourself up in the attic and become a mad poet. You're here, and you simply must participate in the excruciating minutiae of proper housekeeping.

But social interaction inside your home requires only some of your skills. Now we will test the rest. We shall go outside.

12

Public Behavior:
Avoiding Scorn, Dangers, and Museums

*L*et me level with you, dear. It would really be so much easier if you just didn't leave your house. But you will have to.

It's savage out there, lambkin. As Florence Hartley puts it:

> "A lady's conduct is never so entirely at the mercy of critics, because never so public, as when she is in the street. Her dress, carriage, walk, will all be exposed to notice; every passer-by will look at her, if it is only for one glance; every unlady-like action will be marked; and in no position will a dignified, lady-like deportment be more certain to command respect."

"Oh. My. God. Becky. Look at her strut."

Out there roustabouts, gadabouts, and layabouts are lurking everywhereabouts! And they aren't nearly as frightening as the people of quality, all of whom will be eyeing your every step for an invitation to defame your character.

Think of the fun you could have remaining housebound, all the entertainment potential in just taking contemporary medications, trying on your underwear, and berating your servants! Anyway, this desire you have, to explore and adventure, is in itself utterly unfeminine and vulgar.

Really, darling, we could avoid all of this hassle if you would just stay home and take up Montenegrin embroidery. It's a terrific challenge, you know, and no one will try to drag you into a dark alley while you practice it!

No. We can't embrace defeat, can we?

Alas. All right, my dear. Let's hit the street.

How to Be a Street Walker

That right there should be a glaring warning to you. That a term describing the literal act of walking down a street, when applied to a woman, is synonymous with "prostitute." A lone woman, that is. A lady does not walk about unescorted, especially in an urban setting. The most desirable companion is one's own dashing husband. If he is unavailable or nonexistent, there are other ways to maintain a thin veneer of propriety on your ramble. This advice comes to us from the unnamed author of *Etiquette for Ladies: With Hints on the Preservation, Improvement, and Display of Female Beauty:*

"Young married ladies...cannot present themselves in public, without their husband or an aged lady. They are at liberty, however, to walk with young married ladies or unmarried ones, while the latter should never walk alone with their companions. Neither should they show themselves, except with a gentleman of their family; and then he should be a near relation of respectable age."

Loaner crone

Right, then. If you are married, you cannot attend any social function without a husband or a crone. If you do not possess a crone, you may ask the hosts of the social function if they might lend you one. If they do not have a crone and you are married, you may disregard all of the above and just walk by yourself, though to do so is still risky. If you are *un*married, you may *not* walk unescorted with other unmarried girls, as you will be perceived as a sort of roaming brothel gang. The presence of a single married lady, who may or may not be a crone, will mitigate this, and you then may walk as a group. Although you really ought not, unless you can get your brother or father to come, too. It can't be your cousin, because although eugenics is a booming area of study, intermarriage of first cousins is considered acceptable and cannot be considered otherwise as long as Victoria, who bore her (first-) cousin-husband Albert nine inbred children, still reigns over the greatest empire on earth.

"Yeah, I got yer glare right here, matrons."

Now, as to the actual physical movements employed when walking. You are in dreadful error if you think you learned all you needed to know about this subject before the age of two. Yes, you can walk without holding on to the coffee table now, but can you walk so as not to attract lechers and disapproving glares from matrons? *Etiquette for Ladies* suggests the proper way:

"The gait of a lady ought neither be too quick nor too slow....The body and the head should be erect without affectation, and without haughtiness; the movements, especially those of the arms, easy and natural. The countenance should be pleasant and modest."

No. No, that's not right. You must try harder to appear effortlessly unaffected. Heed these instructions from Florence Hartley:

"Do not walk so fast! You are not chasing anybody! Walk slowly, gracefully! Oh, do not drag one foot after the other as if you were fast asleep—set down the foot lightly, but at the same time firmly; now, carry your head up, not so; you hang it down as if you feared to look any one in the face! Nay, that is the other extreme! Now you look like a drill-major, on parade! So! That is the medium. Erect, yet, at the same time, easy and elegant...avoid any gesture or word that will attract attention."

I wanted to offer you an animal as an analogy, such as a gazelle or a cat, to help you capture this feat of unconscious grace, but no such animal exists. Including the human animal. We would have to use computer imaging and a green screen to portray this creature, which is beyond us at this time. Do your best, though. Do not walk fast, slow, firmly, skittishly, with a straight spine, a relaxed spine, a proud face, or a shy face.

Oh, my.

We can still go home and do macramé.

Right now. You say the word and we'll be wearing our leisure corsets and lounging petticoats in front of the fire within the hour.

Heavens. All right. You are an impudent one, aren't you?

Please avoid the following physical movements during your walk:

*These women are violating at least five rules
of proper female street perambulation. Can you spot the
grievous errors that may cost them their lives?*

- Do not turn your head side to side. A loose neck indicates loose morals. Head movement is considered an invitation for men to seduce you. But then again, most everything a woman does risks being read as such an invitation, especially if she forgot her crone.
- Do not stop to look in shopwindows. Staring slack-jawed at feathered hats and pump organs is what a country girl does just before stepping into the wrong hansom cab and being sold into white slavery.
- Do not swing your arms. Bring a parasol to keep yourself occupied. Purchase one if you need to. This might be difficult, as you are not to look into shopwindows to see where parasols are sold.

- Do not—oh, my lands—do *not* dress yourself in public! You are an absolute spectacle, putting on gloves like that. Tying your bonnet string right there on the street! Perhaps you'd like to reach up and give the ol' pantalettes a tug to free them from whatever crevice they've wedged in! Self-respect, darling!

- Do not show recognition of a friend or acquaintance on the other side of the street. There would be no way to greet them without violating a dozen other rules of decorum, shouting and hopping about like an orangutan who sees a bag of peanuts. Pretend you don't see them; they will be pretending the same.

- Do not cross the street unless the street is completely clear of traffic, allowing you enough time to cross without having to increase your speed. A lady does not "hustle," treating all to a free show of bounce and wobble. You must demonstrate the feminine art of patience until the road empties. If you happen to reside in a large city with constantly busy streets, well, that is unfortunate for you.

- Do not look at what is behind you. This is not a metaphor.

- Do not raise your petticoats under any circumstances, no matter how practical. If con-

All right...cross...now. No, stop. Wait. Okay, now. Wait! Don't worry, traffic usually thins out around Christmas morning.

*"Just one little lick...
no one will know!"*

fronted with a mud puddle, a large deposit of animal feces, or a nest of dirty street urchins, it is better to soil your dress than to gratify the perverts lurking in doorways, waiting to get an illicit thrill from the wanton display of your boot tops.

• Do not talk loudly or quickly while walking. Do not laugh while walking. These sounds are like nails on a chalkboard to well-bred men and translate directly to "Kiss me and touch my shins" to lesser men.

• Do not suck your umbrella. I know I've already told you this, but it seems important enough to warrant repeating.

Your Destination

Church. That is your destination. Possibly a sick aunt's mansion.

Etiquette for Ladies reminds us that no woman has any business being alone in a museum, a library, or any other such den of unwholesomeness. Wherever you are going, your behavior once you arrive should remain every bit as self-aware-but-pretending-not-to-be as when you were in transit.

> "When seated, she ought neither to cross her legs nor take a vulgar attitude. She should occupy her chair entirely, and appear neither too restless nor too immovable....It is altogether out of place for a lady to spread out her dress for display, or throw her drapery around her in sitting down, as upstarts do to avoid the least rumple."

Occupy your chair *entirely,* dearheart. One cannot teeter on edge, dangling one cheek above the floor, and still be considered respectable. I'm not sure why you were planning that, but let me stop you before you start.

And though this is not the first nor last time I will remind you, when you are in public, no one wants to hear you talk. You may think you're informed, educated, and intelligent. But to the men who must be subjected to your caterwauling, you are but a frilly little poodle performing tricks on its hind legs.

Just listen to the brave words of another anonymous author, in 1841's *The Young Lady's Own Book: A Manual of Intellectual Improvement and Moral Deportment:*

> "The reputation of being a clever woman is easily obtained. Less than a schoolboy's learning is sufficient to confer it....As to the affectation of wit, one can hardly say, whether it is most ridiculous or hurtful....Who is not shocked by the flippant impertinence of a self-conceited woman, that wants to dazzle by the supposed superiority of her powers? If you, my fair ones, have knowledge and capacity, let it be seen, by your not affecting to show them, that you have something much more valuable—humanity and wisdom."

If only someone had been bold enough to tell this to Harriet Beecher Stowe, before she wrote a book that helped tip our nation into civil war. Or to Ada Lovelace, before she wrote that mechanical algorithm technically making her the first computer programmer. Oh, yes, they and many like them might have changed the world with their "clever" minds, but I imagine they were absolute cankers at parties.

Even if they weren't bores, says our anonymous truthsayer, and

Clara Barton. Ugh. Seated sidewise, spread-out dress, naked hands.
Just because one founds the Red Cross, revolutionizes the profession
of nursing, and saves countless American lives doesn't give one
liberty to sit like a drunk midshipman.

were in fact engaging and entertaining, oh, that could be so much
worse!

After all, "too much fluency and animation in discourse are incompatible with true feminine modesty."

I just can't stress this enough, pet. Men don't want you to "bring
up an interesting point." They don't want you to connect with them
on a cerebral level. They most definitely don't want you to make them
laugh, unless it's because you said something ridiculous in your precious innocence. They want you to smell nice and smile. *The Young
Lady's Own Book* emphasizes:

"That men are frightened at female pedantry [education], is very certain. A woman that affects to dispute, to decide, to dictate on every subject; that watches or makes opportunities of throwing out scraps of literature, or shreds of philosophy, in every company; that engrosses the conversation, as if she alone was qualified to entertain; that betrays, in short, a boundless intemperance of tongue, together with an inextinguishable passion for shining by the splendor of her supposed talents; such a woman is truly insufferable."

Frankly, if pontification is what a woman intends to use her mouth for as she traipses about town, it is preferable that she just go back to sucking on her umbrella handle.

Avoiding Awkwardness. And Kidnapping.

As I have intimated, an unaccompanied lady on the street is all but indistinguishable from a drunken beggar-whore. Who, as in the case above, probably talks too much about philosophy and politics. So, since you had the audacity to leave your home unattended, you ought not to be surprised if men treat you as the kind of woman who has little regard for social mores. Your only weapons are those of decorum.

Poltroons and scoundrels are one thing. We can recognize them and steer clear of their wretchedness. Much more complicated is the proper way to interact with apparently nice men, those who behave politely or even gallantly. There is a very thin line between returning his courteousness and suggesting to him that you desire to hop into his lap and nuzzle his muttonchops.

Says Hartley, "Never stop to speak to a gentleman in the street.

An average street, Bristol, 1890. Full of men.
Prepare to run the gauntlet of creepers and ruffians.

If you have anything important to say to him, allow him to join and walk with you, but do not stop." A moving target is the most difficult to penetrate. Now, regarding which men you may touch. It is highly dependent on weather and visibility. "In the street a lady takes the arm of a relative, her affianced lover, or husband, but of no other gentleman, unless the streets are slippery, or in the evening." Exceptions might also be made for heavy fog, snow flurries, and if you're trying to cop a feel of those rock hard, coal-shoveling wood-splitting horse-reining biceps you suspect lurk under that mackintosh.

"If a gentleman gives you his seat, hands your fare [pays your way], or offers you any such attention, thank him. It is not countrified, it is lady-like. If you do not speak, bow."

You may accept his generosity, but only in such a way that tells him he's so very lucky you deign to accept it. In fact, says Mrs. Hartley, accepting generosity from men is quite ladylike, as long as that acceptance is accompanied by an air of utter disdain for him and all of his filthy gender. Don't worry, he'll respect you all the more for it, if he is of good character.

"There are many little civilities which a true gentleman will offer to a lady traveling alone, which she may accept, even from an entire stranger, with perfect propriety; but, while careful to thank him courteously, whether you accept or decline his attentions, avoid any advance towards acquaintanceship."

The crowded train car: breeding ground of impertinence.

Don't think just because he helped you place your hatbox on a rack on the omnibus that you owe him any favors. For instance, he might try to engage you in conversation. You need to shut that vulgar blackguard down at once.

> "If he sits near you and seems disposed to be impertinent, or obtrusive in his attentions or conversation, lower your veil and turn from him, either looking from the window or reading. A dignified, modest reserve is the surest way to repel impertinence."

Similar precautions may be taken if you are foolish enough to be walking alone on a street, according to *Etiquette for Ladies*. Should some cloven-footed deviant initiate contact with you on the street, tell him to stop.

> "If they persist, she should tell them in a brief and firm, though polite tone, that she desires to be left to herself. If a man follow her in silence, she should pretend not to perceive him, and at the same time, hasten a little her step."

The anonymous author offers no further illumination of what a woman should do if she's being stalked in the night by a strange man, beyond the sly countertactic of walking slightly faster, which is sure to dissuade any predatory behavior. Presumably she should seek refuge in any public place. Well, not a library or museum, we've already covered that. But if she is lucky enough to happen upon a prayer meeting or a tearoom, she can approach another strange man and throw herself on his mercy. Says Hartley,

"If you find yourself, during your journey, in any awkward or embarrassing situation, you may, without impropriety, request the assistance of a gentleman, even a stranger, and he will, probably, perform the service requested, receive your thanks, and then relieve you of his presence."

The necessity of marriage becomes more and more apparent the further we explore the Victorian woman's plight. As she walks away with slightly quickened pace and perfect poise from Jack the Ripper, she hopes only to find another man who, judging solely from his appearance and placement, will not defile her in any way.

Trusting strange men was especially difficult at a time when there was a great fear of white slavery. This term referred to kidnapping innocent daughters and selling them into prostitution, either in the fabled harems of the Far East or the foul brothels of our own cities.

"THE DRUMMER, OR TRAVELING MAN WAY."
When a pander strikes a rural community he must work very smoothly, for every one knows that he is a stranger. He poses as a drummer or traveling man, and seeks the girls in this way, promising a fine time at balls, parties, etc. Once in his power she is lost.

A typical abduction would involve a nice-looking man or often woman (women who committed such vile betrayals against their own sex bore the villainous name of "procuress"). They would strike up a friendship with a restless or lost young girl and then invite her to stay at a friend's boardinghouse they knew of.

The vile procuress

The boardinghouse was invariably a brothel. The girl was immediately violated and had her clothes taken from her except for lingerie. Shamed and ruined, she would be locked into her room and told that she now had to earn her room and board, as well as money to buy new clothes. Thus destroyed both body and soul, the girl could never return home and in fact might never leave the brothel during a life that her broken heart and diseased clients would cut tragically short.

Traveling Man to Man

For a woman to have to travel on her own in the nineteenth century is surely one of the most arduous challenges she shall face, next to living in a war zone and the terrible, terrible surprises waiting for her on her wedding night. Fortunately, Mrs. Hartley is here again, this time to guide her sisters through the treachery of traveling without a man.

First, you need to find a man.

Really any man, provided he is a gentleman. And then give him your money. Your delicate mind was made to calculate the swift geometry of a tidy diaper change and the precise amount of ammonia that will leave your hair *and* kitchen floor scorched free of dirt without blinding your children—not, however, something as mean and heartless as cash.

> "If you travel under the escort of a gentleman, give him as little trouble as possible; at the same time, do not interfere with the arrangements he may make for your comfort. It is best, when starting upon your journey, to hand your escort a sufficient sum of money to cover all your expenses."

You will be man-hopping throughout your journey. You will seek an elderly gentleman to sit next to on the train. You will speak with civility and dignity to the driver of the hack you hire, to the hotel proprietor, to the bellhops. And you will enlist each and every one of them as a temporary husband to help you feel more secure. Even when entering a hotel's adjoining restaurant, it is required that you be escorted, even if only by the waitstaff.

> "Request one of the waiters always to meet you as you enter, and wait upon you to your seat. This saves the embarrassment of crossing the room entirely unattended, while it shows others that you are a resident at the house."

Also remember that choice of dress is of utmost importance for a woman traveling alone.

*The author's own Victorian great-grandmother (right)
and her sister. Dressed plainly enough and properly enough
to travel across an ocean and even briefly become Canadians.*

"A lady will always dress plainly when traveling. A gay dress,
or finery of any sort, when in a boat, stage, or car, lays a woman
open to the most severe misconstruction. Wear always neutral
tints, and have the material made up plainly and substantially, but
avoid carefully any article of dress that is glaring or conspicuous.

Above all, never wear jewelry, (unless it be your watch,) or flowers; they are both in excessively bad taste. A quiet, unpretending dress, and dignified demeanor, will insure for a lady respect, though she travel alone from Maine to Florida."

"You were mistreated? Well, what were you wearing?" That old cliché is not a disgusting relic of primitive misogyny in this century. It is very real. You must be beyond reproach in your modest attire, your quiet and dignified manner, your reasons for indulging in the folly of travel, and even the carefully balanced facial expressions you show. According to *Etiquette for Ladies,*

"But what is especially to be avoided in ladies is, an unquiet, bold, and imperious air, for it is unnatural, and not allowable in any case. If a lady has cares, let her conceal them from the world, or not go into it. Whatever be her merit, let her not forget that she may be a man in the superiority of her mind and decision of character, but that externally she ought to appear a woman.

An affectionate, complying, and almost tender aspect, a tender solicitude for those who are about her, should be shown in a lady's whole person. Her face should breathe hope, gentleness, and satisfaction; dejection, anxiety, and ill humour should be constantly banished."

A woman's face is humanity's finest ornamentation, and all who see it deserve to be rewarded with a view of perfect serenity and innocence.

Now we will look at what happens when that serenity is disturbed.

13

It's Hysterical:
The Least Funny Thing
About Victorian Life

*B*ad news, my fragile flower. This has been a rough trip, and I'm beginning to suspect that you may be suffering the very serious affliction of hysteria. That is to say, it appears your uterus is diseased. Not in any way that we can measure, or test for, or even *see* should we perform one of the increasingly popular "hysterectomies" to relieve you of it. But the sickness is there all the same, and it is causing you to display embarrassing signs of instability. What signs? you ask, a touch of indignation in your voice. You say you're pretty sure you've just got the usual combination of menstrual cramps and a headache?

"Oh, yeah. There it is. Big lump of crazy, right there."

Are you getting lippy with me, Miss Missy?

Hmm. Patient indicates uterine convulsions, cranial derangement, and has been observed displaying impertinent irritability.

Tsk-tsk. Diagnoses confirmed. Hysteria!

Medicinal Orgasms and Other Fictions

So many of the things we've explored in your host century may have caused you to hide a very twenty-first-century smirk behind your gloved hand, for they were silly and strange. But we cannot so easily find pleasure in the oddity that was hysteria. That will not stop us from trying.

Hysteria was not, as you might have been told, a made-up prognosis that sexually frustrated women claimed to have in order to receive medically induced orgasms from handsome doctors. Oh, I'm sure that happened from time to time. All through history, back to Hippocrates, it was suggested that to clear ovarian congestion a midwife should oil her fingers and manipulate the vulva toward a medicinal orgasm for her patient.

And when you add that the nineteenth century is the historical epoch of quackery, you're bound to find a "doctor" willing to perform that technique on you. You could also find a "doctor" to feed you abortion-inducing poisons and cure your ovarian cancer by dunking you in a large pot of Epsom salts and gin. That didn't mean it was generally accepted practice.

Remember, Victorian doctors weren't actually stupid. They were just poorly informed while *refusing to even suspect* that they were poorly informed. At any rate, they didn't think women were incapable of sexual arousal or orgasm. They knew women had orgasms and they

"I'm galvanizing my bosoms so I don't get breastysteria!"

even approved of them, provided they issued from holy marital congress. A wife should be "healthfully sexed" if she is to please her husband and produce broods of fat-legged babies. Those doctors just had no idea *how* women orgasmed. Bless them, they took it for granted that sexual satisfaction in a lady was accomplished the same way it was in a gentleman, which was "Insert male member in specially designed holster, agitate to and fro, repeat, bestow upon female organs the gift of life-giving fluid, and thus share coital bliss." They knew clitoral stimulation resulted in arousal, but that arousal was immature and base, resulting in a puny imitation of the pleasure a woman could receive only when the love pollen of her husband enticed the flower of her cervix to full bloom.

Epilepsy, Cancer, or Maybe You're Just Bored

So let's forget everything we think we know about sex-starved social-ites. They have a place in this era but very little in this chapter. First I would like to tell you what hysteria actually *was*. Which is incredibly difficult. Because the only honest definition I can give you is "a misdiagnosis."

Epilepsy, diabetic shock, neural disorders, post-traumatic stress disorder, postpartum depression, and bipolar disorders do not necessarily cause similar symptoms, but they were all commonly diagnosed as hysteria.

Anything, if it happened to a sullen woman, could be hysteria.

In fairness, the only disease in the above list firmly footed in medical minds of the day was epilepsy. And doctors often wrote of the trouble of telling the two apart. In women, however, secondary symptoms,

The convulsive attack. One potential stage of a hysteric episode.
Or many other dangerous illnesses, some of which actually existed.

such as showing feelings, would often help the doctor diagnose her muscular seizures and unconscious convulsions as a by-product of a temperamental uterus. Or ovaries. Spinal nerves. Brain sheaths? Psyche! Have your bowels been regular?

This is the other reason it is so difficult to tell you what hysteria was. The physical source of the hysterical tendency changed with nearly every doctor and decade of this century.

Hysteria reminds us just how crooked and long the journey to viable treatment for mental illness has been. It is a very *recent* thing that mental illness has a spectrum, a gradient. In 1850, you were a damned lunatic, or you weren't. You didn't vent your insecurities to a talk therapist. You didn't take pills to keep your brain from being so stingy with its serotonin drippings. You didn't even call your mother and moan to her, for she did not raise you to be a blubbering ninny. No!

You usually had two options. By far the most popular was "Quit your bellyaching and get back to the arduous and unrewarding

"Blesh thish fine medicinal whishkey. Keeps me outta the loony bin!"

work of being alive." People who chose this route often also took on the responsibility of self-medication, usually with whiskey or opiates, depending on your income.

Or, you went mad. Screaming-on-the-street-corner crazy. No gradients.

But women, ah, dearheart, we are the weaker vessels. We cannot be expected to mentally bear as much as the stronger sex. Therefore the unspoken historical law, known henceforth as the Kwtcherbitchin Act, held a loophole for the female accused. It was called hysteria.

The Ladylike Version of Crazy

In the 1800s, you couldn't just duck out of life for a week as you might in the twenty-first century. If you were not extremely wealthy, your presence was required for the survival of your family. You couldn't declare it frozen-pizza night and go to bed at seven. Rather, your family would not eat at all if you did not begin laboring for them at sunrise and continue until you dropped exhausted into your bed that night, at which point you would be obliged to roll onto your back and graciously invite your husband to place one more needy dependent at your teat and table.

And if you were wealthy, you had a different kind of pressure, one of appearances and social duties. These were non-optional.

WOMAN

"I'm thinking...I'm thinking I might be over this whole...woman...thing."

Sometimes it got to be too much. Sometimes you had to rest. And since "rest" was for the weak, you had to become weak. You had to *become* very sick.

Hysteria was the perfect kind of lunacy. It left no permanent stain. You could be cured of hysteria—after procuring yourself a nice long rest away from the drudgery of your life. Or, if wealth and position meant your life was simply excruciatingly boring and pointless, you were now involved in the most excitement you'd ever had. Everyone fussing over you, paying attention to your every sigh and twitch. What a far cry from being ignored except for when curtly reminded that proper young ladies do not build towers out of soup bowls at the dinner table. Hysteria was more common among the young and wealthy. They weren't overworked, but their lives were a sort of pointless drudgery, too. Unless they really got off on tatting doilies.

Things You Can Tell Just by Looking at Her Urine

If the hysteria diagnoses did not fall into the category of clearly mistaken physical illness, many of the physical symptoms of hysteria weren't quantifiable. Meaning, you pretty much had to take a lady's word for it if she said she couldn't feel her toes. Even pressing a pin into the affected area to see if sensation was truly dead only required the woman to not express pain, something anyone who's had a booster shot knows is possible.

So when doctors attempted to describe the disease, the result was either a recitation from a *Dictionary of Every Conceivable Discomfort* or a tirade that read like a headmaster's chastising letter home to parents.

Let us look at some of the top medical opinions on the definition of this disease.

According to Dr. John Harvey Kellogg:

"The patient laughs or cries immoderately without cause...
has hallucinations; sensitive to light and sound; breasts sensitive;
pain in ovary; headache; wandering pains in the chest, abdomen,
joints, and spine, especially between the shoulders; loss of sensation in the skin; paralysis of certain muscles; sometimes loss of
voice; sensation as of a ball rising in the throat; contraction of the
muscles; violent spasms; disorder of digestion with symptoms of
nervous dyspepsia; changeable temper; sometimes large quantity
of pale urine; in some cases delirium or stupor."

According to Edward Cox Mann, who wrote 1883's *A Manual of
Psychological Medicine and Allied Nervous Diseases:*

"The mental condition of a woman affected with hysteria is
somewhat peculiar. The patient, when the hysterical feelings
come upon her, does not feel disposed to make the slightest effort to resist them, and yields to her emotions whatever they may
be. She cares nothing for her duties and seemingly takes pleasure
in exaggerating all her slight discomforts and annoyances. She
indignantly resents all attempts and efforts for her comfort and
cure, and discards all advice from her best friends, but will eager-
ly listen to the counsel of the many friends who come in to pity,
sympathize and condole with her."

According to Dr. Pye Henry Chavasse:

"Now hysteria causes a wretched train of symptoms, mim-
icking almost every disease that flesh is heir to. Menstruation in

nearly all cases of hysteria is more or less at fault; it is either too profuse, or too deficient, or absent altogether; so that, in point of fact, hysteria and malmenstruation generally go hand-in-hand together."

As for the poor unfortunate malmenstruating lady, Chavasse says:

"Flatulence is sometimes the torment of her life; it not only causes much discomfort, but frequently great pain. The wind wobbles about the bowels outrageously; first, in one place, then in another, then rising in volumes to her throat, almost choking her the while.

There is another peculiarity of hysteria which is very characteristic of the complaint, namely, a hysterical patient is afraid to go either to church, or to any other place of worship. If she should venture there, she feels as if she should be smothered or suffocated, or as though the roof were going to fall upon her; and, at the sound of the organ, she is inclined either to swoon away or to scream outright."

"I say smirk—they say face half paralyzed by hysteria."

So, a quiet, moody, achy, cranky, overly emotional, church-dreading, pale-pee malmenstruate with gas so intense she actually seems to be choking on it.

We know something these men seemingly did not, *cherie.* We know that probably every woman who ever existed has had a day or twenty that could be described in those terms. Except for choking on your own internal flatulence; that would be quite an ordeal, worthy of medical study. Otherwise, what he's describing is just a lousy, hormonal weekend.

Faking and Feeding

It's not that these women were faking their misery. They *were* unhappy, as humans who have the time and leisure to consider their condition often are. The problem was all the circumstances that were feeding that unhappiness.

The mind can wield heavy power over the body, and a woman taught her whole life to believe the words of educated men over her own instincts would have a highly suggestible brain. Women were encouraged toward "hysteric behavior" by the doctors who treated them and the loved ones who worried for them. A deep sigh becomes a moan, which elicits attention. The moan rises to a shriek. The shriek, to be fair, is long overdue in a culture that punishes human expression. And smashing the pillows with your fists feels awfully right, too. Cathartic. And all the while the doctor is nodding his head, his suspicions confirmed, and your usually distant mother is wringing her hands in despair over you.

One author, George Junkin Preston, who wrote *Hysteria and Certain Allied Conditions, Their Nature and Treatment,* makes the observation that the more restrained a culture is, the more likely you were to see cases of hysteria, manifested in sudden bursts of emotion, crying, laughing, and hugging strangers. He suggests hysteria was the mind and body compensating for the lack of emotion permitted in civilized society. You couldn't get any more emotionally restrained than the nineteenth century, *while* still having access to romantic novels and sweeping tales of adventure and magazines filled with beautiful lives that it was becoming increasingly apparent you weren't going to have.

Dr. Mann gives a harsh but likely accurate portrayal of the emotional hysteric.

> "We must endeavor to remove the mental or emotional cause of the disease. The class of patients whom we see are women, who, from their social position and surroundings, have really no object in life but to amuse themselves. They have, as a rule, been spoiled and petted since childhood, and as their nervous system is developed far in excess of their physique, they become, as they grow up, capricious and hysterical.
>
> Their imaginary ailments are undoubtedly the cause of much distress to them, for to a person with highly strung nerves a slight pain seems a severe pain, and discomfort is magnified into pain.
>
> One of my last cases, who had an income of six thousand

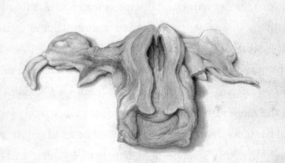

The culprit. Look at it. It verily screams treachery.

dollars, and who had nothing to do, and who had consequently become an aggravated case of hysteria, would have been, as a physician who was also a patient with me, remarked, 'a splendid woman if she had to live on twenty-five hundred dollars a year.'"

Whom Shall We Blame?

The woman. Don't be stupid. The woman, of course. The chances she is innocent of inciting this condition are quite slim. Even if she's epileptic, it's likely a blight God delivered unto her for some secret vice. The better question is, why have all these women suddenly chosen to *become* blighted? As the century wound down, there were proportionately fewer cases showing indisputable medical symptoms (physically ill women were becoming more identifiable as such), and there was an increase in cases of women who complained of varied, intense, but completely invisible symptoms. It was almost as if it had become a fashion for women to lose their self-control. What was causing this?

Dr. Kellogg believes hysteria stems from dirty thoughts and luxury and wishes women could partake of all the fine health inherent to southern slaves:

> "It is a notable fact that hysteria rarely or never occurs among the women of uncivilized nations. It is stated that before the war, the disease was unknown among the Negro women of the South, though it has occasionally been met with since the emancipation."

Really? Physicians weren't called to attend slave women who refused to get out of bed or wouldn't stop crying? Of course, physicians

Mary Brice was a slave who lived in a town named Lynchburg. And no, no, she never complained of hysteria.

probably were not often called to attend slave women who couldn't stop vomiting blood, either. Again we are faced with the possibility that data regarding nineteenth-century minorities might be biased or incomplete.

Dr. Chavasse pins the blame for the current hysteria for hysteria on partying too much, 1800s style.

"There is among young wives, of the higher ranks an immense deal of hysteria. Can it be wondered at? Certainly not. The fashionable system of spending married life, such as late hours, close rooms, excitement, rounds of visiting, luxurious living, is quite enough to account for its prevalence.

The menstrual functions in a case of this kind are not duly performed; she is either too much or too little 'unwell;' 'the periods' occur either too soon or too late, or at irregular periods. A fashionable wife and happy mother are incompatibilities! Oh! it is sad to contemplate the numerous victims that are sacrificed yearly on the shrine of fashion!"

There you go again, you defiant wretch of a girl, shirking menstrual duties so you can stay awake past 11 p.m. and flit around fashionable parlors. If you entertained half as many people inside your uterus as you do in your drawing room, as Nature commands, you probably wouldn't be having health issues.

Late nights, fashionable clothes, and an ice cream parlor.
To think they honestly didn't see that the eventual consequence
of their lifestyles would be mental derangement!

There was, of course, one more enormous, unspeakable cause of hysteria. One horrifying enough to require its own chapter, that we may prevent its foulness from contaminating the perfectly innocent subjects that surround it.

The Cure
(Still *Not* Sexy Doctors or Orgasms)

You're still very much hoping the cure is some sort of accidental-on-purpose masturbation, aren't you? Our modern culture loves that idea. How loathsome. Put your petticoats back on, you devious coquette. The cures you'll be enduring are remarkably less lusty.

First of all, most doctors insisted the patient be removed from her home before any treatment could begin. Even then, many doctors sensed that a hysteric condition was egged on by those who indulged it.

Says Dr. Preston:

"One great reason why the treatment of hysteria is so much more successful in institutions than at home is, because in a hospital or sanatorium absolute obedience to the rules is insisted upon.

The daily life of the patient should be arranged for her; for example, it is well to write out a schedule upon which is set down the hour of rising, the time and character of the meals, the periods for rest and exercise, and like details. The establishment of regular habits that are carried out with martial exactness is the first step in the treatment. It is well to inquire minutely into the daily routine of the patient's life, and impress her with the importance of the various measures instituted."

Strictness, rules, yes. That's fine; any high-society Victorian knows how to follow rules. But these rules have a *real* purpose for once! These rules aren't about remembering how long your husband's white cuff should extend from his sleeve to differentiate him from the man who delivers your coal! These rules will change her life! And these rules mean someone is *taking care of her.*

For the first time since she was fourteen, she's not responsible for all the burdens Victorian womanhood casts upon her. If she's rich, she doesn't have to change clothing four times a day and repress every urge that would cause the world to suspect she's flesh and blood, not carved of finest, coldest marble. If she's not rich—oh, heavens. She needs a break. She needs to no longer slowly come undone under the weight of so many responsibilities in a brutal world. And with hysteria, all she has to do is eat her mush, take her nap, and get electricity zapped to various parts of her body. (No, not the fun parts. Stop that.)

Still, some cures were quite nice, like the massage technique Preston recommends:

> "Massage should be practised upon the bare skin. It may be said, in general that there are the following important movements: (1) Pressing and kneading with the finger-tips or knuckles. (2) Tapping with the hand, fist, or some mechanical contrivance. (3) Pinching, which is performed by picking up the muscle-bundles that can be grasped."

He instructs that this begin at the toes and continue on over the whole body except the face. He could be subtly recommending knuckle-tappy, pinchy, nurse-delivered masturbation, but if he is I'm not sure you're meant to enjoy it. You would, however, probably enjoy an entire body massage, and it would likely help almost anything that ailed you, real or imagined.

Kellogg demands that the general health of the patient first be improved through fresh air, exercise, and food conducive to predictable and amicable bowel movements. He is also a fan of water treatments. This primarily meant interrupting a woman's paroxysm (not the orgasmic kind, the screechy, wailing kind) by pouring freezing water over her head and down her spine. Which I bet worked incredibly well for all versions of hysteria not involving actual brain trauma. Becoming markedly enraged at the thug who would drop a bucket of water on your addled brain would likely eclipse most any other emotion.

Even better, though, was the extremely newfangled use of electricity. Says Kellogg: "Galvanism to the spine is another useful measure. When there is paralysis of sensation and motion, faradic electricity should be applied to the paralyzed parts."

FIG. 29.—GENERAL FARADIZATION (SECOND STAGE).

Electric shocks can make dead frogs dance, you know. They should be more than sufficient to convince a young woman she can feel her feet again.

Then the combination of electricity and massage hit the market in the form of, yes, early electric vibrators. They were very popular among doctors who specialized in nervous disorders and quacks who specialized in bored rich ladies. The real doctors did not advise that the device, called a faradizer, galvanizer, or simply the Hammer, be used on genitals. Don't use something called the Hammer on your private parts. You ought not even need to be told that.

Instead they recommended applying the vibrations directly to the affected area (in the case of hysteria, the region of the abdomen over the ovaries) or, more commonly, the spine.

Joseph Mortimer Granville marketed one of the first electronic vibrators. In his 1883 medical treatise/instruction manual *Nerve-Vibration and Excitation as Agents in the Treatment of Functional Disorder and Organic Disease,* he states that nerves

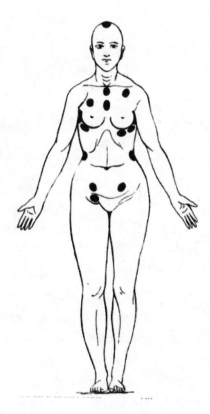

Pressure points to which to apply vibrators to relieve different nervous illnesses. Note the decidedly nonsexy ovarian position for hysteria.

which cause trouble, such as the ones that induce hysteria in women, are like particularly stupid soldiers. Their electrical pulses are vibrating out of rhythm. It is the job of his electric hammer to be the sergeant who teaches loafing lady-nerves to march straight.

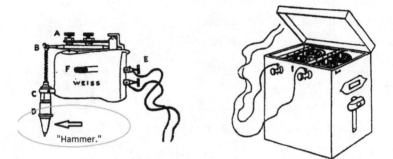

Granville's original "hammer" vibrator
with battery supply, circa 1880s.

"The manner of operating is to apply the flat-headed hammer, if we have to deal with a deeply-placed or large nerve sheath, the pointed hammer if the nerve be superficial or small, the hard brush if several nervous filaments lying close together are affected, or the disk if the area of superficial disturbance be very large; and to keep up the percussion until the jerking, twitching, or spasm, reflexly excited by the vibration subsides."

This certainly sounds dirty, but he does not ever explicitly say that "the percussion" should be applied to the genitals. He, like others working medically with electricity, believes there were spots on the spine that corresponded with urogenital organs, and they should be the spots receiving the hammer blows. And in the cases where the doctor thought the uterine tract was congested...with...whatever miasmas and vapors do so poison a hysterical woman, a variety of vaginal douches, from light warm spritz to the freezing-cold fire hose, was recommended.

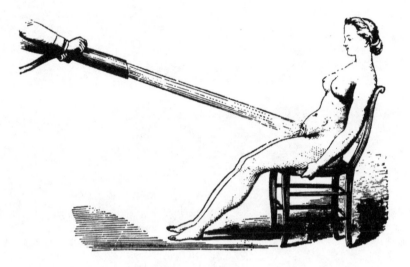

*The fire hose of hysterical relief. Apparently aimed at the
abdomen, but wherever works best.*

Are you terribly disappointed we didn't fully examine the masturbation cure? Do you think the method deserves consideration?

You are in luck. Victorian men gave masturbation, and the women
who might employ it, a *great deal* of consideration. And so shall we.

Prepare for shame.

14

The Secret Vice:
"Where Warts and Tiny Nipples
Come From"

*B*ack in the twenty-first century, masturbation was a personal choice. Many of us in the Western world give it no more significance than scratching an itch. Our beloved partners could scratch it better, perhaps, with the special rhythm we've developed together through trial and error. But, should they have already fallen asleep or in fact not exist, well, many of us keep our own back-scratchers by the bed.

Still, some of us believe the habit to be unhealthful, and we spend our most sensuous and hormonal years burying the urge or sating it with substitutes, like 1960s-era musicals and imported cheeses. We may consider it a religious transgression, or we may believe it just isn't good for us.

Fewer of us believe it will give us finger warts, turn our breasts small and sloppy, and strike us down with bona fide catatonia. We're pretty sure it can't drive us mad or make us sterile. And we'd be downright shocked to find ourselves dead from it.

Not so in the nineteenth century. Self-abuse, or masturbation, was considered terrible for your health and your happiness. That is one of the main reasons I believe electric vibrators were never professionally employed by scrupulous doctors to combat *any* female ailments. Those doctors believed it was masturbation that *caused* all those ailments.

What Is It, and Are We Certain It's Bad?

Oddly enough I found little evidence that anyone ever asked this question. That doesn't stop Mr. Fowler from answering it. And so to ease any awkwardness, let *us* be the ones to pose the question. Mr. Fowler, is masturbation unhealthy for females?

"Must our girls by millions thus palsy their whole female nature and offspring by masturbation, and virgin victims by the hundred thousand crowd her house whose steps take hold on hell? The very flower of their sex die off thus polluted? Must such vast numbers adapted to be our best wives and mothers—earth's greatest blessings—become our worst vampire harpies? Each some one's daughter, and but for their fall, luxurious wives and mothers of future millions?"

Polluted…hell…vampire harpies… hmm. I believe our distinguished man of letters is saying "Yes. Masturbation is not healthful and ought to be avoided."

Why? Well—simply look at Nature as it exists around you and do the math! Or let Mr. Fowler do it for you!

"By requiring both sexes to cooperate in creating life, Nature forbids all amatory action of men with men, women with women, man with himself, and woman with herself, and commands that all amatory action shall be between a male and female."

Mademoiselle Ch., young female aged fifteen, before the effects of masturbation

This works in much the same way as by requiring dirt to grow food,

*Mademoiselle Ch.,
age sixteen, after the effects
of masturbation*

Nature expressly forbids the eating of pie on top of hay bales. Pretty obvious, really.

Most anti-masturbation advocates believed masturbation was *not* something a person learned naturally. The idea of a small child ever finding cause to touch herself above the knees and below the navel was preposterous! All the good bits are outside this equator of sin, darling! Your throat for beautiful hymn singing! Your arms for filling out pretty puffed sleeves! Your feet for walking very quietly so as not to increase Mother's suffering from her sick-headache! Therefore masturbation was considered something taught by bad people to innocent ones. Fowler weeps for the trials that await the pure child.

"A covered, slimy, filthy, poisoning slough underlies your paths, more vile than can be described, destructive to all your rosy cheeks, your happy hours, your life-long joys and powers, from whose fatal blight you can never free yourselves. It is Masturbation, or self-pollution, and consists in handling your private parts while indulging vulgar sexual feelings, by imagining impure pleasures with your opposite sex. It is taught by bad boys and girls, and worse men and women, often by nurses, learned the most in day and boarding schools, academies and colleges; and practiced almost universally from five years old up."

Women working at a Heinz canning factory. With each turn of the machine they become more and more depraved.

He even names the women most likely to indulge in it.

> "Almost all factory operatives of both sexes learn and practice it. French drug stores sell an invention used expressly and only for female masturbation. A grass widow [a woman abandoned by a bored husband] owned leaving two husbands because she preferred this solitary vice."

Heaven defend us. Divorcées? French textile workers? The very worst of the worst.

Death by Masturbation: What a Way to Go

I feel obligated to mention, my sweet friend, that here we are going to wade around in the shallowest waters of a black and bottomless swamp. Victorian attitudes toward masturbation splash about in the ridiculous, but take one step out too far and the lake bed plummets from under you; you'll find yourself cracking your skull on the jagged bedrock of shame, mutilation, and unspeakable cruelty. If you knew the things I know, you'd never be able to eat a bowl of Kellogg's cereal again; just having to stare at the family name would make you snap, crackle, and pop with rage.

In fact we may start with Dr. John Harvey Kellogg. He was absolutely convinced that nearly every female malady that didn't come from clogged bowels came from masturbation. (The original cornflakes, incidentally, were invented to help combat *both*.)

In his 1881 book, *Plain Facts for Old and Young,* we are told just some of the life-threatening conditions this habit caused in women and girls.

- Ulceration About the Roots of the Nails and Finger Warts. Caused by the fingers' constant contact with the "acrid, irritating secretions of the vagina." Acrid? *Acrid?* It's not a Venus flytrap, sir, oozing acids to dissolve the flesh of its struggling prey!
- Uterine Disease. This vague diagnosis results from constant "congestion" of a sexually stimulated womb. Also it was believed that women engaged in clitoral, vaginal, and *uterine* masturbation. I could not find a record of how we might go about exciting our uteruses to a sexual frenzy; I can only picture a woman slapping her own belly pink in the privacy of her chamber and feeling very let down by the results.

- Cancer of the Womb. "Degeneration of this delicate organ also occurs as the result of the constant irritation and congestion, and is often of a malignant nature, occasioning a most painful death." It's uterine cancer, madam. You have three agonizing months to live. But you rather brought it on yourself, didn't you, trollop?

- Sterility and Frigidity. "A total loss of sexual desire and inability to participate in the sexual act, is another condition which is declared by medical authors to be most commonly due to previous habits of self-abuse." Here we have an example of a very simple principle that doctors like Kellogg never

John Harvey Kellogg.
Don't be fooled by that sweet face.
That's how he lures you to
his enema machines.

seemed to consider in their "research." Causation versus correlation. Does masturbation *cause* sexual disinterest? Or do the two merely correlate, perhaps due to some wild, unexamined factor, like the lackluster ministrations of a now-snoring husband?

- Menstrual Derangements. He just has to use such *dramatic* words for common things. "Heavy-flow days." There, is that so hard to say? Must a woman's period be likened to an escaped mental patient wielding a shiv carved from a spoon?

- Precocious Puberty. Puberty is not considered precocious by modern medical standards unless it sets in before the age of eight. The Mayo Clinic of the twenty-first century helpfully lists all the information it has about the condition, which is extensive, on its website. Then, regarding the factors causing precocious puberty that it hasn't decoded, it does something truly fantastic. The leading medical minds of our generation say, "We don't know why." How much pain was caused and progress thwarted by the Victorian medical community's unwillingness to say those four words? It's so much easier to blame the unknown on the unseen.

- Prolapsus and Various Displacements of the Female Organs. I'm sorry, Dr. Kellogg, but I refuse to believe that I can masturbate my private parts until they fall off me. They simply cannot be that loosely attached.

Sorry, Venus—those itty-bitties might have worked for Botticelli, but Kellogg knows what you've been up to.

- Uncontrollable Itching That Leads to Public Masturbation. "Continued congestion produces a terrible itching of the genitals, which increases until the individual is in a state of actual frenzy, and the disposition to manipulate the genitals becomes irresistible, and is indulged even in the presence of friends or strangers, and though the patient be at other times a young woman of unexceptionable modesty." The doctor himself hasn't ever seen this happen. But this other doctor wrote him that some patient's mom heard about it. From their neighbor. She lives in Canada. You don't know her.

- Small Breasts. Oh, dear. You used all your sexual power to clog up your filthy bits and there was none left over to make a bosom. Oh, that's a shame. Oh, and look, just about every woman in your family for generations was a chronic masturbator, too! How else to explain this disturbing trait repeated so often? And don't try that old "I am as God made me" line on me, Miss Busy Fingers. Do you *really* think He intended you to have a body shape that varies from the one I personally find most attractive?
- Atrophied Breasts. Another term for when a breast loses fatty tissue and begins to droop. Caused by chronic masturbation. Or, by having breasts.
- Spinal Conditions. Fine. Sure. Toss that on the pile.
- Nervous Disorders, Insanity. "But in females the greatest injury results from the nervous exhaustion which follows the unnatural excitement. Nervous diseases of every variety are developed. Emaciation and debility become more marked even than in the male, and the worst results are produced sooner, being hastened by the sedentary habits of these females, generally. Insanity is more frequently developed than in males." This of course includes hysteria, which encompasses any diseases missed on the preceding list.

It is not fair of me to spit such vitriol without allowing you, my intelligent companion, some explanation. I won't burden you with details, which are found abundantly in Dr. Kellogg's many books on women's illnesses and the personality flaws that cause them. But I will give you his prescribed treatment to cure nymphomania, defined as "a condition in which there is such an intense degree of sexual excitement that the passions become uncontrollable. A female suffering with this affection will sometimes commit the grossest breaches of chastity. Its principal causes are self-abuse and a complete abandonment of the mind to lascivious thoughts."

To the unchaste woman he deigns to suggest this treatment:

"Cool sitz baths; the cool enema; a spare diet; the application of blisters [carbolic acid] and other irritants to the sensitive parts of the sexual organs, the removal of the clitoris and nymphae [labia minora], constitute the most proper treatment."

He also recommends it for masturbators.

"The same measures of treatment are indicated in the cases in which the disposition to practice self-abuse is uncontrollable by other means."

Please remember his medical advice on self-abuse was intended for women *and girls*.

Darling, as we have gone on this journey together, we have always endeavored to keep an open mind. We have often been baffled by the past, even wryly amused, but we have made an effort to not condemn the people who lived in it for the 150 or so years of knowledge they hadn't acquired.

I suspend this rule on this topic and this man.

Because this isn't the slow and invisible accumulation of white lead, or the ever-with-us vanity of trying to cut a fashionable figure. This is brutality in an age proud to have outgrown that designation. Simply put, this time, they should have known better.

I shall try to communicate my feelings in the most ladylike and reserved manner of which I am able. I simply hate you, Dr. Kellogg.

Among a century's worth of questionable medical practice toward women, your quackery takes the sugarless, spiceless, fibrous cornflake *cake.* As much as Mr. Fowler might rave at the moon, you are worse. Because you had power. You are horrible, misogynistic, and too busy designing new enema attachments to be attentive to the thousands of patients putting their lives in your famous hands. If you were on fire I would not urinate on you to extinguish your agony, not only because it would be but a portion of the pain you'd inflicted on others, but also because I'm sure that instead of gratitude you would have me committed for flagrant display of my peculiar "peeing on immolated jackasses" fetish.

Signs of Secrets

Oh! Do wait. Though we may not trust Kellogg (who tells us that we should suspect any little girl "showing excessive fondness for mustard, pepper, vinegar, spices, and other stimulating condiments" and that "little girls who are very fond of cloves and desire to be always eating them are likely to be depraved in other respects"), we always try to heed the stark truths our Mr. Fowler hurls at our heads. There are many ways, he tells us, to spot the telltale signs of the woman who practices the secret vice.

Your daughter shows an interest in making cookies? Cookies with spices?

She complains of being cold. "Nothing equally robs
    the system of animal warmth, and causes icy-
    cold hands, feet and skin; just as a right sexual
    state warms."

She has trouble with her gravel. And consumption, of course. "This
   drain induces costiveness, liver complaints, gravel difficulties
   [kidney stones], dyspepsia, consumption &c, by breaking down
   the weakest organs, and inducing death in the name of other
   diseases."
She feels sad and achy and has trouble with her pee. Her self-abuse
   "induces a gnawing, faint, sunken, gone, distressed feeling
   around stomach and heart, and morbidity throughout. The
   urinary function suffers most."
She has tiny nipples, etc. Doing you-know-what "...dwarf[s] the
   sexual organs of both sexes, testes, penal, mammal, pubic, and
   pelvic, nipples included..."

Somehow it is much more palatable coming from Fowler. I respect a
man who believes his message is so important that he can't bother with
standard punctuation.

Sin or Insanity, But Seldom Both

One thing Kellogg did do that I can reluctantly commend: he at least
made sexual information, however wrong, available to the common
person. Few were doing that. In fact, it was often argued that topics of
a sexual nature should be discussed exclusively by medical men and
religious leaders in Latin. Only men of the highest caliber could read
Latin in the nineteenth century. Well, men with rich fathers who sent
them to fine colleges. But that was pretty much the same thing at the
time.

Therefore, heated debates of whether or not accidentally getting an
erection should be a confessable sin were intelligible only to the pru-

rient-minded, as no sexually malformed individual would be capable of retaining a language of such holy beauty in their diseased minds. (Shush, you.) The famous German physician Carl Capellmann, who wrote 1879's *Pastoral Medicine,* a book intended to help priests figure out dilemmas just like that one, wrote mostly in English, reserving Latin for only the dirtiest of mental word-pictures (such as words that translate into "impure touch"). And no, by the way, it was not a sin as long as the erection was accidental. As for women, they do not become accidentally stimulated, says the doctor. But they *do* often tell him that they use masturbation to ease internal pain.

That should be no surprise, says the doctor. Lust *is* pain.

"Such patients often assert, amongst other things, that they experience relief from pain through practicing self-abuse in a more or less complete way (pressing or rubbing of the clitoris, etc.). It may, indeed, appear so to the patient, for pain and lust meet each other, and may alternate in hysterical persons, whose nervous system is so much perverted; but this can never make self-abuse allowable to these patients."

Even if the woman in question is not seeking or receiving sexual gratification from this act, she is absolutely seeking and receiving sexual gratification from this act. She is sinning and must be penitent.

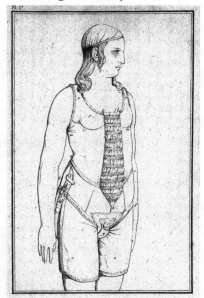

Antimasturbation device for use in insane asylums

Unless her masturbation habit has rendered her an idiot—too crazy to understand sin.

> "These practices, as resulting from a morbid condition of the body, may not appear sinful to them, but they are, nevertheless, materially, an unnatural and illicit gratification of the sexual instinct. The priest cannot allow it; but, should he think the psychical conditions of the patient changed to such a degree that the sin cannot be imputed to her, then she is only so far responsible as she may have been originally guilty of causing or encouraging her abnormal condition; and her case no longer has its place in foro conscientiae, but must be subjected to the treatment of the physician of the insane, and must invariably be referred to him."

She's still on the hook for the masturbating she did *before* she went insane, however. And never be fooled by a woman who is too bashful to spread her genitals before a physician while saying, "My priest said I'm abusing myself so much I'm going to go insane, could you take a look?" If a woman winces at the thought of that encounter, she's all but signed her own confession.

> "The pretext of repugnance to medical examination and consultation should not be easily credited. A *really* chaste woman will be made so unhappy through the condition above described, and will detest the desires and practices of self-abuse arising therefrom to such a degree, that she certainly will not refuse a decent medical consultation, if she is told that she may entertain a well-grounded hope of being in this way freed from her physical affliction and moral danger."

You Can Wash It. Once.

In their 1889 publication, *Sexual Health: A Companion to "Modern Domestic Medicine,"* Henry G. Hanchett and Alexander Hamilton Laidlaw break the unfortunate news that our vaginas are so troublesome we're bound to be miserable no matter what we do with them. Even if you're a good girl and never, ever, *ever* touch it, well, much to our astonishment, that can prove to be equally unhealthy.

"Young girls frequently have so impressed upon them an idea of the shamefulness of touching the privates, in fact in some cases almost of the disgrace of having privates at all, that cleanliness of those parts is neglected with far worse than ordinary consequences. It not infrequently happens that persistent itching and discomfort, nervousness, irritability, peevish restlessness, discontent, melancholy, and even mental disturbance [occur] in girls and unmarried women who have been taught never to touch the privates."

This can be remedied. But if you didn't want to touch it before, oh, dear. You're really not going to want to now. A woman's vaginal complaints "may be completely cured by simply separating the

"Doris! Step away from the washtub before I clout you again! It hasn't been a full week, you can't wash it yet! I'm trying to help you, Doris!"

larger and smaller lips that are found on either side of the vagina, and cleaning out from the furrow between them a mass of cheesy matter, the accumulated discharge of the glands at that point."

Oh, dear. Oh, heavens.

And to make sure the problem doesn't recur, one must bathe that insidious troublemaker. At least once a month.

> "So greatly have very serious symptoms been benefited in so many cases by this simple procedure that it must be thought an important matter to instruct girls and women to separate these lips and wash between them at least once a month, and in warm weather—say from May to November—as often as once a week."

Society made women so terrified of their own bodies that they were too scared to wash an area in glaring, odorous, and painful need of it. After all, if you had been taught that your vagina was dirty, it wouldn't surprise you to find that it was actually dirty, would it?

Oh, gracious. I do believe that whole chapter was just one big fit of hysteria.

I am beginning to see why they were so popular.

Conclusion:
I Miss Pants

*C*ome sit beside me a moment, my dear, dear friend. How are you faring? It's not been easy, has it?

I will confide in you something I'm sure you've already guessed. It wasn't quite as bad as all this. What I've shown you is all true, but it did not apply to everyone, always. Just as today not every woman undergoes radical plastic surgery so she can join Hugh Hefner's harem, not every woman ate arsenic, crushed her bones with a corset, or woke up in a cold sweat fearing she'd put her soup spoon on the wrong side of her cheese fork at dinner the night before.

But neither was it as you've been told by books and movies. The beautiful dresses were smudged with soot and sweat. The succulent feasts were made from questionably preserved plants and unrefrigerated animal products, then prepared by unwashed hands. And though you might have been treated like a lady, it would come at the expense of being treated like a woman.

Of course it wasn't all foot rubs and mint juleps for men. Their lives, even with subservient women, could be just as doused in suffering and hardship. But they *were* less affected by horrendous hygiene, magical-thinking medical care, straitjacket wardrobes, and positively shatter-pated social mores.

Western civilization in the twenty-first century: it's not perfect, but it's pretty good. Compared to what our great-great-grandmothers knew, it's more than good; it's a fairytale land of luxury, freedom, and gender equality. They didn't live to see it, but they started it.

We have this world in part because those Victorian women began to apply pressure to the walls that trapped them. One million women nudging at the same time over a long period can create profound movement.

They couldn't all be Margaret Sanger or Clara Barton or even Charlotte Brontë. But they could—and many did—take every opportunity to prove themselves strong, intelligent, and worthy. I know I wouldn't have done any better than my great-great-grandmother. She was kind, tough, and smart. She had a daughter whom she raised to be kinder, a little tougher, and smarter. And so on down the line to me, and to you, each generation wiping away one more layer of patronizing grime from the minds of their descendants.

And that's why you and I can wear pants. And run for president. And divorce men who hurt us. And do whatever work we want or need to do to make our lives as we would have them.

Oh, pants. I miss pants. And underwear made from high-performance synthetics. And human rights. Yes. I'd like to go home. Will you accompany me? We can come back here any time. All our favorite movies and books are waiting for us, and they will still present their best for our enjoyment. Oh, we know it's just for show, but that doesn't mean it isn't lovely.

Come on. We'll grab some fat-free froyo, text our partners to remind them they promised to make stir-fry tonight. We'll fill a shopping cart to spilling with safe, effective ibuprofen and tampons and shampoo. Just because we can.

ACKNOWLEDGMENTS

HUGS!
Word Hugs! TO:

*T*o my mentor, Chris Higgins, who made this all happen. There was an impassable chasm between who I was and who I wanted to be, and he single-handedly built the rope bridge across it and walked with me step-by-step the whole way. He didn't have to, but he did. Also he keeps my Ro warm at night.

To Jessica Papin: She can move the earth and sky and everyone in the New York Port Authority with the sweet silver that comes off her tongue. She moved this dang book in two days.

To Jean Garnett: My God, you believed in me. And you worked so hard. An editor who stays up past midnight matching jokes about chamber pots to their corresponding images while telling me I make Shakespeare look like a turd. Thank you for flattery, faith, and ferocity. Turns out I need all those real, real bad.

To Tiffany Hill: Thump them all over the head with it.

To Molly: Every girl needs an imaginary sex-librarian friend.

To Alison Southwick and Dr. Matthew Anderson: Thank you for letting me sit with you in the cafeteria. Thank you for still loving me, nonstop, for twenty weird years. And for not being remotely surprised about all this.

Acknowledgments

To Mrs. Lois Simmons: You were the person I was writing to in my head. An absolute lady in every regard, but not one to be squeamish. Thank you for loving me so long and so strong.

To Maren Bradley Anderson, who wanted to be a writer and so became one. Then told me to quit whining and be one, too.

To all the Shed Girls: Thanks for laughing on cue. You're my best nerds.

To Lisa: My wizard with a tool belt. You changed everything. Don't you ever get sick of being right?

To Jayne Yaffe Kemp and Deb Jacobs: Copyeditors don't get enough love. Without you guys I'd just have a three-hundred-page underwear rant on my hands.

To my babies: LE, Brubby, Mason-boy, and Little Birdie. I love you.

To Mom and Dad: Just...couldn't have hung around a tad longer to see your kid write a book about old-timey vaginas, huh? Always, I am writing for you.

To Gus: All you ever wanted was to be left alone. But every time I'd come to you with something new and awful that my career trajectory would do to your dream of living in a cave on the dark side of the moon, you'd smile and say "Great!" You are my heart and my head and my husband. If ever two were one. Stay cool and have a rad summer.

Bibliography

Alcott, William A. *The Young Wife, or Duties of Woman in the Marriage Relation*. Boston: George W. Light, 1837.

Anonymous. *Beauty: Its Attainment and Preservation*. New York: Butterick, 1892.

———. *Cassell's Household Guide: Being a Complete Encyclopaedia of Domestic and Social Economy, and Forming a Guide to Every Department of Practical Life*, vol. 1. London: Cassell, Petter, and Galpin, 1873.

———. *Etiquette for Ladies: With Hints on the Preservation, Improvement, and Display of Female Beauty*. Philadelphia: Lea and Blanchard, 1840.

———. "Sentimental Toilets." *The Tomahawk!* (March 3, 1796).

———. *Sylvia's Book of the Toilet: A Ladies' Guide to Dress and Beauty, with a Fund of Information of Importance to Gentlemen*. London: Ward, Lock, 1881.

———. *The Toilette of Health, Beauty, and Fashion Embracing the Economy of the Beard*. Boston: Allen and Ticknor, 1833.

———. *The Toilette, or A Guide to the Improvement of Personal Appearance and the Preservation of Health*. London: John Dicks, 1854.

———. *The Woman's Book Dealing Practically with the Modern Conditions of Home-Life, Self-Support, Education, Opportunities, and Every-Day Problems*. New York: Charles Scribner's Sons, 1894.

———. *The Young Lady's Own Book: A Manual of Intellectual Improvement and Moral Deportment*. Philadelphia: John Locken, 1841.

Ashton, James. *The Book of Nature: Containing Information for Young People*

Who Think of Getting Married, on the Philosophy of Procreation and Sexual Intercourse; Showing How to Prevent Conception and to Avoid Child-Bearing. Also, Rules for Management During Labor and Child-Birth. New York: Wallis and Ashton, 1861.

Bank, Mirra. *Anonymous Was a Woman: A Celebration in Words and Images of Traditional American Art—and the Women Who Made It.* New York: St. Martin's Griffin, 1995.

Beeton, Isabella. *Beeton's Book of Household Management.* London: S. O. Beeton, 1861.

Betts, B. F. "Symptomatic Indications of Remedies for Subinvolution of the Uterus." *The Hahnemannian Monthly* (March 1889): 190.

Buck, Albert Henry, ed. *A Treatise on Hygiene and Public Health,* vol. 1. New York: William Wood, 1879.

Capellmann, C. *Pastoral Medicine.* Translated by William Dassel. New York: Fr. Pustet, 1879.

Carson, Gerald. *One for a Man, Two for a Horse: A Pictorial History, Grave and Comic, of Patent Medicines.* Garden City, NY: Doubleday, 1961.

Chavasse, Pye Henry. *Advice to a Wife on the Management of Her Own Health and on the Treatment of Some of the Complaints Incidental to Pregnancy, Labour, and Suckling, with an Introductory Chapter Especially Addressed to the Young Wife.* New York: John Wurtele Lovell, 1880.

Culverwell, Robert James. *Medical Counsellings, or The Green Book: The Modern Treatment of Syphilis...and All Diseases of the Urinary and Sexual Organs.* London: Published for the author, 1841.

Cunnington, C. Willett, and Phillis Cunnington. *The History of Underclothes.* London: Michael Joseph, 1951.

Ellington, George [pseud.]. *The Women of New York, or The Under-world of the Great City.* New York: New York Book Co., 1869.

English, V. P. *The Doctor's Plain Talk to Young Men: Anatomy, Physiology and Hygiene of the Sexual Organs by V.P. English, M.D.; Inspired by His Infant Son.* Cleveland: Ohio State Publishing, 1895.

Fowler, O. S. *Private Lectures on Perfect Men, Women and Children, in Happy Families: Including Gender, Love, Mating, Married Life, and Reproduction, or Paternity, Maternity, Infancy, and Puberty.* New York: E. W. Austin, 1880.

Bibliography

Glasse, Hannah. *The Art of Cookery, Made Plain and Easy: Which Far Exceeds Any Thing of the Kind Yet Published.* London: Printed for J. Rivington and Sons et al., 1784.

Granville, J. Mortimer. *Nerve-Vibration and Excitation as Agents in the Treatment of Functional Disorder and Organic Disease.* London: J. and A. Churchill, 1883.

Hanchett, Henry Granger, and A. H. Laidlaw. *Sexual Health: A Companion to "Modern Domestic Medicine"; A Plain and Practical Guide for the People in All Matters Concerning the Organs of Reproduction in Both Sexes and All Ages.* New York: C. T. Hurlburt, 1889.

Hartley, Florence. *The Ladies' Book of Etiquette, and Manual of Politeness: A Complete Handbook for the Use of the Lady in Polite Society.* Boston: Lee and Shepard, 1872.

Hernandez, Gabriela. *Classic Beauty: The History of Makeup.* Atglen, PA: Schiffer, 2011.

Hoff, Charles A. *Highways and Byways to Health.* St. Louis: Planet Book Houses, 1887.

Horan, Julie L. *The Porcelain God: A Social History of the Toilet.* New York: Kensington, 1997.

Hudson, George W. *The Marriage Guide for Young Men: A Manual of Courtship and Marriage.* Ellsworth, ME: Published by the author, 1883.

Incognita [pseud.]. *Toilet Secrets.* London: J. C. Bridgewater, 1869.

Jameson, Helen Follett. *The Woman Beautiful.* Chicago: Stevans and Handy, 1899.

Jay, William. *Thoughts on Marriage: Illustrating the Principles and Obligations of the Marriage Relation.* Boston: James Loring, 1833.

Jefferis, B. G., and J. L. Nichols. *Search Lights on Health: Light on Dark Corners; A Complete Sexual Science and a Guide to Purity and Physical Manhood, Advice to Maiden, Wife and Mother, Love, Courtship, and Marriage.* Naperville, IL: J. L. Nichols, 1895.

Keith, Melville C. *The Young Lady's Private Counselor: The Care of Mind and Body; A Book Designed for Young Ladies, to Aid Them in Acquiring a Life of Purity, Intellectual Culture, Bodily Strength and Freedom from Many of the Ills and Annoyances of Life That Custom Has Placed on the Sex.* Minneapolis: Buckeye Publishing, 1890.

Kellogg, John Harvey. *Ladies' Guide in Health and Disease: Girlhood, Maiden-hood, Wifehood, Motherhood ... Illustrated.* Des Moines, IA: W. D. Condit, 1884.

_____. *Plain Facts for Old and Young: Embracing the Natural History and Hy-giene of Organic Life.* Burlington, IA: Segner and Condit, 1881.

Mann, Edward C., and William J. Mann. *A Manual of Psychological Medicine and Allied Nervous Diseases, with Especial Reference to the Clinical Features of Mental Diseases, and the Allied Neuroses, and Its Medico-legal Aspects, with a Carefully Prepared Digest of the Lunacy Laws in the Various States. Designed for the General Practitioner of Medicine.* Philadelphia: P. Blakis-ton, Son and Co., 1883.

Meigs, Charles D. *Obstetrics: The Science and the Art.* Philadelphia: Lea and Blanchard, 1849.

Montez, Lola. *The Arts of Beauty, or Secrets of a Lady's Toilet.* New York: Dick and Fitzgerald, 1858.

Montgomery Ward and Co. *1894-95 Catalogue and Buyer's Guide.* Edited by Joseph J. Schroder. Reprint, Chicago: Gun Digest, 1970.

Morrow, Prince A. *Social Diseases and Marriage; Social Prophylaxis.* New York: Lea Brothers, 1904.

Napheys, George H. *The Physical Life of Woman: Advice to the Maiden, Wife and Mother.* Philadelphia: David McKay, 1888.

Papachristou, Judith. *Women Together: A History in Documents of the Women's Movement in the United States.* New York: Alfred A. Knopf, 1976.

Pearl. "Snares for Spinsters. By One of Them." *Monthly Packet* 89 (1895): 491.

Power, Susan C. Dunning. *The Ugly-Girl Papers, or Hints for the Toilet.* New York: Harper and Brothers, 1874.

Preston, George J. *Hysteria and Certain Allied Conditions, Their Nature and Treatment, with Special Reference to the Application of the Rest Cure, Mas-sage, Electrotherapy, Hypnotism, Etc.* Philadelphia: P. Blakiston, Son and Co., 1897.

Rayne, M. L. *Gems of Deportment and Hints of Etiquette: The Ceremonials of Good Society, Including Valuable Moral, Mental, and Physical Knowledge.* Detroit: Tyler, 1881.

Ruth, John A., and S. L. Louis. *Decorum: A Practical Treatise on Etiquette and Dress of the Best American Society.* Union Publishing House, 1882.

Sears, Roebuck and Co. *1902 Edition of the Sears, Roebuck Catalogue.* Reprint, New York: Bounty Books, 1969.

Shoemaker, John V. *Heredity, Health and Personal Beauty.* Philadelphia: F. A. Davis, 1890.

Smith, Virginia. *Clean: A History of Personal Hygiene and Purity.* New York: Oxford University Press, 2007.

Sozinskey, Thomas S. *Personal Appearance and the Culture of Beauty, with Hints as to Character.* Philadelphia: Allen, Lane and Scott, 1877.

Tomes, Robert. *The Bazar Book of Decorum: The Care of the Person, Manners, Etiquette and Ceremonials.* New York: Harper and Brothers, 1870.

Tuttle, James P. "Cosmetics, Their Constituents and General Effects, with a Few Special Cases Other Than Saturnism." *The Medical Record* 25 (March 8, 1884): 257.

Walker, A. *Female Beauty, as Preserved and Improved by Regimen, Cleanliness and Dress and Especially by the Adaptation, Colour and Arrangement of Dress.* New York: Scofield and Voorhies, 1840.

Walker, Alexander. *Woman Physiologically Considered, as to Mind, Morals, Marriage, Matrimonial Slavery, Infidelity and Divorce: With an Appendix, Containing Notes and Additions.* New York: J. and H. G. Langley, 1840.

Warren, Ruth. *A Pictorial History of Women in America.* New York: Crown, 1975.

Warren, Stewart. *The Wife's Guide and Friend: Being Plain and Practical Advice to Women on the Management of Themselves During Pregnancy and Confinement, and on Other Matters of Importance That Should Be Known by Every Wife and Mother.* London: Lambert, 1900.

Wehman, Henry J. *The Mystery of Love, Courtship and Marriage Explained.* New York: Wehman Brothers, 1890.

Wood, James C. *A Text-book of Gynecology.* Philadelphia: Boericke and Tafel, 1894.

About the Author

Therese Oneill lives in Oregon and writes humor and rare-history articles for many different outlets, including Mental Floss, the *Week,* the *Atlantic,* and Jezebel. She can be found online at writerthereseoneill.com.